RED ROSE PARANORMAL

Everyday paranormal tales
and classic cases from Lancashire

RED ROSE PARANORMAL

Everyday paranormal tales
and classic cases from Lancashire

STEPHEN WADE

This paperback edition published in Great Britain in 2014 by DB Publishing, an imprint of JMD Media Ltd

ISBN 978-1-78091-418-3

Printed and bound in the UK by Copytech (UK) Ltd Peterborough

CONTENTS

ORDINARY AND EXTRAORDINARY TALES

EERIE DISTURBANCES IN THE WORKPLACE

ACKNOWLEDGEMENTS

Thanks go to a number of local historians, correspondents and librarians for help with gathering the material for this book. For some of the Liverpool tales, Richard Whittington-Egan's writings were invaluable. As a general store-house of stories, John Roby's classic collection, Traditions of Lancashire (1900) was a wonderful source of stories from all quarters. Also, that extensive treasure house of Lancashire history, the Transactions of the Lancashire and Cheshire Antiquarian Society were very useful. Otherwise the sources were random and fortuitous, as so often happens in paranormal stories. But helpfully, The Fortean Times, Ghost Voices and other periodicals have collections of readers' stories which were of great value to me.

Also behind all paranormal narrative and research there are the massively influential figures of Peter Underwood, Frank Podmore and Colin Wilson, amongst others. But of unusual and special value from all the classic writings has been the recent (2010) update of Andrew Green's This Haunted Land, undertaken by Bowen Pearse and published as Ghost-Hunter's Casebook. Mr Pearse has very thoughtfully updated Green's earlier investigations, and so his writing on Smithins Hall and Samlesbury Hall have been very useful indeed.

Of course, there will always be the words 'Pendle Witches' whenever we think of paranormal Lancashire. The folklore and traditions relating to these witches extends far into past writing and storytelling. In 1845, a writer in an antiquarian journal explains that at that point the stories and beliefs were very much still alive:

' Pendle forest, in the neighbourhood of Burnley, has long been notorious
For its witches. No fewer than ten of the residents of that locality suffered
The extreme penalty of the law at Lancaster in August, 1612 and one died
In prison.....Two hundred years have since passed away, and yet the old
Opinions survive; for it is notorious that throughout the Forest the farmers
Still endeavour to
'Chase the evil spirits away, by dint
Of sickle, horse-shoe, and hollow flint.'

Pendle figures in this book, but in a limited way.

Classic early investigations by the Society for Psychical Research have provided the basis for some accounts also, but at the base of all work done there are the 'everyday paranormal' tales of people who sent stories, so thanks to all those, including Ken Wenlock in particular.

For the Blackpool tales, I am indebted to the research and writings of Darren Ritson, whose work in northern ghost experience contains arguably the definitive guide to Blackpool's restless dead. For many contemporary investigations, thanks go to all the local paranormal groups across the county whose reports I have used and found fascinating. All the groups who spent time in pubs and manors looking for material have proved to be a great help.

PREFACE BY IAN LAWMAN

Presenter of Living with the Dead

If I had to choose a paranormal focus of activity in the county, it would have to be the Blackpool experience. As soon as Stephen told me he was writing on Lancashire I thought of that place. On one occasion I led an investigation at The Spanish Hall there and we had faces in mirrors, moving glassware and a sight of a former workman who met a tragic end there – and of course Charlie Cairoli. I have to explain that Charlie is my spirit guide. Charlie, who was the former Tower Circus clown, has been my guide since I was very young. There is more on this in Stephen's section on Blackpool here.

When I investigated the Spanish hall I had twenty guests, and we spent the night behind the stage and in the Baronial Hall. In the Spanish Hall there are some clouds hanging from the ceiling and I saw a man doing some maintenance work up there on the lighting rig. I actually saw him falling to his death. He had been hanging on to one of those clouds while someone ran to get help, but sadly he lost his grip and fell. It was quite emotional to see; we found out from a local historian that a maintenance man had died working in that room. It was very sad.

I had been working with Stephen Mercer, the marketing manager of the Grand, and he invited me to come up and spend the night. We even did some 'scrying' – which is an old Victorian parlour game, using mirrors.

All in all, Blackpool's mysteries make it unforgettable, and that would be my own Lancashire paranormal hot spot. There are plenty of other locations across the county with so many amazing stories attached, but Blackpool surely has something unique in this respect. The zoo there also has a history of paranormal activities, and I have conducted ghost walks there and at Louis Tussaud's Waxworks. I recommend a visit to Blackpool for anyone with an interest in what we call 'the paranormal' – those aspects of life we can't really explain by our reason. The place has given me some truly memorable times, and I'm sure there is always room for another Lancashire collection.

Stephen's new survey of stories will provide something new and something old, in that he has looked again at some legends or established places and also added accounts from everyday life. I find this a good read and I'm sure you will.

INTRODUCTION

Like my other books in this series, the unique element of my collection is that I mix established stories from the county with correspondence and other reports from everyday experience. This means that there is no particular stress on the use of scientific hardware and gadgets, though these are mentioned where relevant; there is little detailed analysis of findings as in some periodicals, and most of all there is the emphasis on the story and the storyteller to take centre stage. For the older, circulated tales, I have relied on a range of sources, some classic; but for a large number of others, the sources are scattered. I'm sure that the mix I offer will be like no other comparative collection.

Matters paranormal have progressed somewhat since Dr Johnson's definition of a ghost in his 1755 Dictionary of the English Language: he simply wrote, 'The soul of man.' He did add, quoting Shakespeare that a ghost would hate anyone who 'upon the rack of this rough world/stretch him out longer.' But essentially, science had come to our aid. The only reservation on that score is that it must never pretend to have all the answers.

It was the poet, Coleridge who said that he did not believe in ghosts because he had seen too many of them. He added that the very evidence for their existence was that there was a lack of evidence. Put more simply, we might say, there is no smoke without fire. The whole business of paranormal visions is clouded by a whole spectrum of matters, from medical illness, to visions and hypnagogic states (that consciousness we have when half asleep and think we see things), and from 'corner of the eye' phenomena to repeated perceptions confirming earlier experience of others. Yet in spite of this we go on ghost-hunting, and as Peter Ackroyd noted in his social history of ghosts, 'The English are obsessed with the past, with ruins, with ancient volumes... Ghosts therefore may be seen as a bridge of light between the past and the present, or between the living and the dead.'

The towering figure of John Roby stands behind any book on Lancashire folklore. He was born in Wigan in 1793 and although he started as a banker in Rochdale, he was a natural raconteur, and we have a glimpse of him from Edwin Waugh in his book, Lancashire Sketches, from the time Waugh worked in a bookshop:' For the clergy of the district and for a certain class of politicians, this shop was the chief rendezvous of the place. Roby used to slip in at evening, to have a chat with my employer and a knot of congenial spirits who met him there. In the days when my head was yet a little way higher than the counter, I used to listen to his versatile conversations.'

Roby embellished, of course, being a product of the Romantic period, but his books were influential on those writers who came later. He thought of himself simply as a collector of oral tradition, explaining his setting and aims in this way:' In the northern counties and especially in Lancashire it may readily be imagined that a number of interesting legends, anecdotes, and scraps of family history are floating about...preserved in the shape of oral tradition...' Well, my book is unashamedly about the anecdotes 'floating about.'

His death was as dramatic as his tales; he died in a shipwreck in 1850 when SS Orion struck rock at Port Patrick on its way from Liverpool to Glasgow.

Some regions of Britain gather a certain distorted image with regard to the folklore of hauntings. Sometimes this comes from modern investigations, so that Suffolk will always mean Borley rectory to many readers; Yorkshire generally means Bollings Hall and sites in York, and Lancashire is forever now a word immediately suggesting to many the Pendle Witches and that celebrated episode of Most Haunted with Derek Acorah and the team firmly in the grip of malevolent spirits. Yet that tale is embedded in a fully sourced historical narrative; the origins and evidence there are easily checked and verified. That is not always the case, and my collection of Lancashire hauntings will offer, inevitably a mix of established and new cases. One thing they all have in common is best expressed in the words of Carl Jung: ' There are strange and wondrous things in these lands of darkness.'

In all paranormal tales there are always the frustratingly brief accounts of things, such as the supposed 'choked battallion' and their ghostly footsteps at Newton-le-Willows. Tradition has it that these footsteps are the sounds of the Highland soldiers captured by Cromwell's men in 1648. The prisoners were hanged, with little ceremony. But there lies the frustration with such matters – 'tradition has it...'. The details are a snippet, no more. The search has to be for stories with a trajectory, a development, even if there is no closure.

Lancashire has no shortage of haunting tales; these go far beyond the witches and the people trapped in various hiding places when recusants were hunted down. The halls, manors, pubs and taverns are packed with unexplained stories allegedly from the shadow world. Previous surveys of the county by folklorists and social historians have brought out several surprising locations, but once again, television has made a few notable places more prominent, such as the psychic Derek Acorah's experience at Brannigan's club in Manchester; but the paranormal magazines in recent years have also featured Lancashire locations, and a typical example of this is the fascinating account of Sunlight House by Steve Mera, to whom I owe the story.

John Roby, as previously mentioned, embodies the kind of writer who grew up among the Lancashire legends. As his publisher wrote of him: ' In his immediate vicinity were Haigh Hall and Mab's cross, scenes of Lady Mabel's sufferings and penance...almost within sight of his windows lay the fine range of hills of which Rivington Pike is a spur...' I cannot claim to have that background and a 'local habitation' as Shakespeare expressed it. I have come to know many stories from the county from friends and fellow writers, though thirty years ago I had the pleasure of knowing the illustrious writer from Great Harwood, Joan Pomfret, and in fact my first printed piece of prose was in one of her anthologies, Betwixt Thee n' Me. Other confrontations with tales from the county have come to me via writers and friends, notably Richard Whittington-Egan, the chronicler of Liverpool.

Lancashire has a long tradition of antiquarian scholarship and some of my sources lie deep in the byways of that literature, expressed in countless memoirs as well as in the pages of the Transactions of the Lancashire and Cheshire Antiquarian society. The Lancashire Dialect Society literature has also been useful. Paranormal narratives today exist somewhere between folklore motifs and stereotypes, and the first-hand experience of those who love to disseminate the unexplained in life. My stories come from that meeting-point, and although I am aware of the new methodology, and the discipline fired by scientific gadgets in such research, I still have to stick close to the traditional starting-point of 'It is said that...' and 'I saw something I can't explain but I saw it with my own eyes...' Collections recently gathered by The Fortean Times and by countless web sites give testimony to this expansion of interest in the anecdotal story- the half-felt, uncertain perception explained after the event with caution and doubt, but with an underlying belief that what happened was beyond the scope of the rational mind to understand.

There is one difficulty in retelling actual witness accounts of a ghost experience: it competes with the fictional ghost story. Both the factual and the fictional have one thing in common, though, as Susan Hill has described the fictional: '

Atmosphere is essential to a ghost story. How does it come about? By evocative description and a sense of place -perhaps the traditional empty haunted house at night. Buildings are important. But a deserted office block at night in an empty city centre could be a place full of ghosts..' Susan Hill has here hinted at one of the obstacles to the success of the real ghost story - the settings are often quite banal. But we still have to believe that the fearful sensations of the actual experience will lift the factual into competition with the fictional.

The range of experiences in my collection also reflects the continuing miscellany of the alleged communications with and from the dead; for instance, new terminology has come along to explain some of these, such as lithobolia for the occurrence of falling stones, events related to the falling coins as in one of my stories. In relation to this breadth of phenomena in a haunting, there has been an increase in the level of media interest, and in an odd way, Lancashire has to some extent avoided this. In a list of TV series devoted to regional hauntings within the last five years, Lancashire locations do not figure prominently.

In the end it has to be said that this county has so many entrenched tales, from oral history rather more than from the 'urban myths' category that what tends to happen is that local investigators and writers tend to work intensively in their neighbourhood, so that there are clusters of local tales in the tracts of rural Lancashire, and then there are town specialists who find more than enough in their urban locations, such as Manchester,

Liverpool and Blackpool, as obvious examples. The number of local paranormal investigation groups has multiplied recently, as television has made investigations into the unknown popular. In relation to that we have also had the growth of what is called 'urbexing' – exploring the dark and often subterranean locations across the land. That had linked, or taken in, a certain amount of ghost-hunting and there has been an increase in examples of so-called paranormal visual evidence caught on camera and displayed ion the internet.

As for traditional Lancashire, its endless resource of legend as well as modern everyday ghost sightings will always have plenty to offer, and new experience comes along all the time. In the Victorian years, the press tended to laugh at ghost stories, and they liked nothing better than to report a tale like this, which was based on an actual climate of fear in this particular Lancashire village:

'There is a ghost in Lancashire. Garstang is its exact location for the
Present. Between the railways station and the village it walks at night in
White, terrible to mortal eyes. Such, at all events, is the conviction of
Mt Fawcett's intelligent subordinate in Garstang, the postman, who has
Just proved the strength of his sense by resigning from his office and
Seeking a more congenial and less nocturnal sphere of usefulness remote
From the railway station. Also the young men of Garstang move about at
Night only in gangs armed with cudgels. A daring sceptic has suggested
To the police that 'some young fellow has been enfolding himself in a

White sheet and parading the road… In the meantime it is to be hoped that

The school board of Garstang will endeavour to get the children past

Standard IV as soon as possible.'

This is the kind of story that prompts a genuine paranormal investigator to answer back. But the point about the Victorian attitude such as that is that the adopted and popular mindset of pinning everything on sound rationality opens up such fear that abuse and ridicule hide a set of insecurities, and there is nothing like a really genuine and inexplicable haunting to melt the tough exterior of the rational sceptic.

To sum up: we tend to laugh and ridicule tales of haunting through fear more often than through genuine objective thinking; a writer on matters occult can only assemble what has been stated and recalled. Of course memory is fallible and of course psychology has theories and explanations for all perceived phenomena. We have 'perceptual sets' which means that our minds put meaning together from limited stimuli, using past experience, so a flapping piece of tarpaulin on a branch at dusk is seen as a 'ghost.' But that is reductive, closing all other avenues of thought, and hauntings experienced over time, by several people, show the limits of that line of thought, however persuasive it might be on individual cases.

Part I

HALLS AND MANORS

As one social historian wrote in 1910: 'At the baronial hall, the ghost is a cherished, petted heirloom.' That is something the writer on ghostly halls, manors and abbeys is always up against as a potential hurdle in the way of credence. But the stories are there so we press on and try to understand as well as re-tell the tales. We expect a manor or an old family home, where aristocrats or industrial barons have lived to have a resident ghost; it goes with the fittings. But this is down to the media and the heritage industry rather than to paranormal investigation and writing on the subject.

Halls and manors have their very own unearthly feel: they provide the stock locations for fictional horror tales and they often seem forbidding and daunting simply by their appearance - all that old timber and creaking floors, windy corners and dank cellars. Reports and investigations do not have to work hard to bring these places into paranormal scenarios, and the following provides merely a selection of the places with dark reputations across the county. Almost every valley has its Gothic history akin to the classic contexts of rural folk tales and hearsay.

At the heart of the interest in these locations is the 'stone-tape theory' as explained by Peter Underwood: 'This is the idea that scenes or events from a place's history become trapped in one spot and that years later those snatches from the past are spontaneously rerun, like a video-tape, and can be heard or seen by witnesses, is at the very least a plausible and convenient idea...'

This would seem to be easily applied to places which have dark, enclosed and solidly walled areas, and of course, places such as cellars and central rooms in mansions with a large number of rooms on different levels. Underwood also adds the interest in the idea of 'dominant individuals' from the past taking part in 'traumatic events.' All this adds interest to the combination of stone and thickly walled places together with murders and suicides within the confines of the building.

THE WARDLEY HALL SKULL

Wardley Hall is an early medieval manor house in Worsley, Greater Manchester. There is no set law that manor houses should have resident restless spirits, but he ghost alleged to dwell within has a right to be restless, if the old belief that tormented souls dwell in the place where their lives were cruelly taken away. The ghost in here is that of Father Ambrose Barlow, an unfortunate victim of the savage punishment of hanging, drawing and quartering in which England used to excel as specialists in inflicting horrible pain. The tale if of a skull – something that is a recurring motif in paranormal history and writings.

Father Barlow suffered this death for keeping to his faith, dying in 1641. As was the custom in those times, his head was displayed supposedly at Manchester church, and then traditional tales have told that the skull was brought to the Hall by a fellow Catholic later, and hidden. In the eighteenth century the skull was found by a servant, and she (perhaps sensibly) hurled it into the moat. But there was reputedly a storm after that and the disturbance was out down to the removal of the skull. Of course, there must have been some decisive action taken, because the moat would have to be drained so that the skull could be found. If so, there must really have been a sense of terror in the house.

Another tradition is that a man called Roger Downs, a ruffian and a killer, was the person from whom the skull was taken; being a troublemaker, he picked a fight with a man in London and his head was severed in the scrap. Both origins make good stories. What does not encourage further credence to the tale is the fact that skulls preserved and taken from the Hall have not later been associated with any unexplained and disturbing consequences.

HAUNTING AT THE OLD MANOR, BOOTLE

This old manor house in Bootle was built in the sixteenth century, but in 1941 the Horner family planned to buy it and establish a shop and tea-room there. The history of the place was eventful, being yet another place that Cromwell has 'messed about a bit'

Frances Horner has written about what happened there after she started planting flowers in the garden. What she found was a beautiful brooch with a porcelain mosaic pattern. There was nothing strange about that, but shortly after that she was disturbed in her sleep and she got up and walked to the window, looking out over the garden. She looked around and saw that, strangely, the outside door was open - and she had locked it earlier. Poor Frances then recalled what happened next: a man came into her room; he had white lace at his throat and his wrists and he had a candle stick in his hand.

The figure seemed to float past her and disappear. She turned the light on and, as we would all do in the circumstances. She did not sleep but sat with the light on, sat on the bed, but then stretched her hands and caused some plaster to come loose. She could not explain why, but Frances ripped more plaster and paper away and there was a hollow space emerging, and then a shelf. On the shelf was a candle stick. She must have felt her heart pound at that point. But more treasure awaited her: she found a brooch again, and a small stone box in which there was an ear-ring and some glass beads, a buckle, a ring and some coins.

When she woke up next morning, she explained about the plaster and said that she knew a candle and bible would have been kept in the space behind. To her relief, her mother said that, a short while previously, she too had seen an apparition. The two women said nothing to the father in the house, and it was all quietly pushed aside.

Frances joined the navy shortly after this and time moved on. In her memoir, she wrote that, naturally, she always wondered what happened to the little treasure hoard she found, and if the ghost was still active afterwards. Was it, she speculated, the spirit of the man Cromwell had victimised and robbed of his worldly goods - all except the little cache on the shelf?

SAMLESBURY HALL GHOST

When a location is a regular on the tourist map, we should lament the fact that investigations and experiences will not be taken seriously. But Andrew Green's account of this hall, between Preston and Blackburn, includes a footnote of great interest.

The story is that the ghostly presence there is that of the daughter of Sir John Southworth. Her name was Dorothy and her appearances follow the established pattern of unhappy spirits haunting places of great tragedy: her lover was murdered in the sixteenth century, and he was buried by the outer wall. There the murdered man has been seen, moaning. The couple intended to run away together, but that her lover was a member of the rival Hoghton family and there was an ongoing feud. Dorothy's brother killed the man, and his sister was rushed away to a convent where she soon wasted away and died. A writer of earlier times wrote that after Dorothy's death, 'on certain clear and still evenings, the apparition of Dorothy Southworth, clad in flowing white, was said to be often seen gliding along the gallery or through the corridors into the hall. She would descend the staircase or through the corridors into the hall.

This has elements of legend, but Green's footnote forty years ago was that during drainage work around 1970, workmen found a skeleton, a male one. Recently, Bowen Pearse has updated Green's summary, and he adds the information that the hall was rebuilt in the sixteenth century, after Thomas

Southworth inherited the place in 1517; he was a Catholic, and during the persecutions, Pearse points out, he hid people and made priest-holes for the protection of hunted men and for escape should a mass be discovered.

A later Southworth, John, was High Sheriff of the county, but even he had to tread carefully in matters of belief. During one raid in the mid sixteenth century, a man Southworth was hiding was discovered and killed. Allegedly, blood still appears in the priest hole from time to time

But the earlier ghosts are not the only presences. Pearse tells of a Victorian shade, one Joseph Harrison, who was the owner in the 1870s. If accounts are to be believed, this character is a playful spirit who even harasses young women.

What of Dorothy though? Pearse has more to add to the main Samlesbury ghost. He notes sightings: 'she has stopped buses on the nearby road an then disappeared; she has done the same with motorists... another tale is that a police car hit a lady in white.' Apparently, she also made an appearance before two soldiers stationed near the Hall, and Pearse notes that one suffered a 'seizure.'

There are now frequent investigations of the place by paranormal groups, and there is always the danger as a consequence that the determination to see, record or monitor such a well established presence may lead to all kinds of doubtful material, but the search has to go on. The questions always need to be asked, and even Green himself commented at one point that there is no trace of Dorothy in the Southworth family tree.

John and Anne Spenser have a report of their own to add to the Samlesbury story. Their account of the place notes that there had been 40 reports of a white-cloaked lady seen by drivers, and they explain one typical sighting, by Alex Dunderdale and his wife in November, 1987. Mr Dunderdale, as the car drew near the hall, saw a white lady in front of him and he braked quickly. Then, 'Mr Dunderdale searched the road for her injured or dead body but could not find her. His wife had not seen the woman but felt the car lurching as it had apparently run over her... He searched for over half an hour but returned to the car, no less frightened and shaken than when he left it.'

They add that even pedestrians had seen her: '... one or two people walking down the road after having missed the last bus have seen her appearing or disappearing in front of them.'

Samlesbury also has the tale of Sykes's Wife. There was a lonely farm out on Mellor brook, close to the hall, and this had been owned by the Sykes family for centuries. Back in the fifteenth century the Sykes couple who lived there were infamous as miserly types; word spread around that their cash was hidden somewhere in the farm, because they earned but never spent anything. The couple died, about the time of Richard III, and nobody was told where their money was hidden. A new tenant moved in.

Shortly after that, the new owners began to see the apparition of the old lady, described as a very old woman wearing scruffy clothes- 'wrinkled garb' as people said. The most fearful aspect of the sight of the old Mrs Sykes was that her ghost always walked with head down looking at the ground, without making a sound. She was seen in the barn as well as in the house, and once she stood by an old apple tree. Time passed, new tenants came, and still her ghost was seen and reported. One sighting described her: 'She had a withered face, with short and quaintly cut gown. With a striped petticoat and a crooked stick... at first she was not there, as I was near the tree, but as soon as I plucked an apple... there she was!'

Then one day, as the owner of the farm was well into a drinking session, her ghost appeared and he had the courage to ask her why she was always troubling his home. She walked out and stopped by the stump of an old apple tree. It was in an old part of the orchard, an area which had not been used for many years. The farmer was sure that this was something important, the fact that she stopped there. He had heard the tales of the hoard, and so he dug down on that spot, and the coins were found. Tradition says that when the last jar was brought up, an unearthly smile went over the face of the old lady and the ghost faded away, never to be seen again.

Samlesbury Hall: a hotspot of paranormal activity from an old print

SMITHILLS HALL PRIEST APPARITION

As with Samlesbury, Bowen Pearse revisited the place and its story to revise Andrew Green's writings in the 1970s. The Hall is on a site at first established by the Knights Hospitallers and its long life, with many different phases, ended with its purchase by the Corporation of Bolton in 1938. The record of the earlier occupants is clear: William de Radclyffe took over from the Knights, and then it was enlarged by Andrew Barton in 1516.

The Hall passed through many hands and so there have been countless people coming and going through the centuries, but generally the ghost there is thought to be that of George Marsh, and once again, this is a story of persecution, He was one of the many who suffered at the hands of Queen Mary. The network of recusants and rebels meant that he had warning of the arrest, but his mother was held hostage. He was tried for heresy. He asked God to know the justness of his cause and looked up to heaven.

Going through the chapel, as he walked to his death at the stake, he is supposed to have stamped a foot in anger, and hence we have the so-called bloody footprint there. Green reported a sighting of a cleric in the green room. But again, Bowen Pearse has expanded and reconsidered the stories.

Pearse has discovered than there was a celebrity visitor to the Hall – American novelist Nathaniel Hawthorne, in 1855. He apparently was convinced that there was something paranormal about the print, noting, ' The footstep seemed fresh, as if it had been that very night imprinted anew and the crime made all over again, with fresh guilt upon somebody.'

John Roby tells the tale of George Marsh in some detail, in his collection published in 1829, and he adds this anecdote:

'The stone was once removed for a frolic by two or three young men who lived in the house. Taking advantage of their parents' absence, they cast it into the glen behind the hall. That same night, on retiring to rest, the inhabitants were disturbed by many strange and hideous noises. Much alarm and inquiry being excited, the offenders confessed, and the stone was restored to its place with great reverence and solemnity...'

Roby also is clear on the judgement and death of the unfortunate Marsh: ' From Lathom, where he was examined before Lord Derby and his council, and found guilty of heretical opinions, he was committed to Lancaster and from thence to the ecclesiastical court at Chester, where, after several examinations by Dr Cotes, then Bishop of the diocese, he was adjudged to the stake and burnt in pursuance of his sentence, at the place of execution near that city, on the 24th April, 1555.

If we need to check on more recent experiences there, Bowen Pearse once more has a tale to tell. He relates what happened on a tour of the Hall;

a woman in the group was taken ill, and the guide went to her and put his hand on her shoulder. Pearse writes: ' He later described how it was, a terrifying icy sensation comparable to nothing he had felt before or since... Somehow, his intervention seemed to break the spell that held the woman enthralled...' The woman later said that she had seen a woman's face – 'it was like the years fell away and I was staring into a mirror.'

Smithills Hall always seems to live up to its reputation.

'A PRESENCE' AT SPEKE HALL

Speke Hall is a fifteenth century manor house, now run by the National Trust, a magnificent structure with the distinctive black and white timber work we associate with the Tudor age. Its ghost is agreed to be that of Mary Norris, who inherited the Hall from her uncle in 1791. She married Lord Sidney Beauclerk, a noted rake of the time, fond of gambling and having a good time. He continued his dissolute ways even up to the time when Mary was pregnant.

One day he shocked her by announcing that he had lost everything they owned and that their future was ruined: disaster faced them. Mary decided on suicide, first hurling their young child from a window and then going to the great hall to commit suicide. Her spirit haunts the tapestry room. A typical sighting is that recorded by Adelaide MacGregor who said that she had seen a translucent figure walk across the room and then disappear in a wall. A secret passage has been found in the wall where the figure went.

The last private owner of the Hall was someone called Watt, and at one of her dinner parties the group of guests saw Mary's ghost again, walking into the wall. But there is doubt here, as there so often is. There is no real evidence that the Beauclerks lived at the Hall. But Andrew Green has commented: ' But, as P W G Lawson, assistant keeper of the Hall, points out,

" am inaccurate story does not reflect on the validity of the room as a haunted site.‚Äù' The guide told Green that a lot of visitors had reported seeing a figure in the tapestry room.

BRADSHAW HALL POLTERGEIST

A special exhibition at Turton Tower recently was of great interest to anyone interested in the paranormal. There, some objects have been exhibited that create a stir, both in legend and in the real sense of unease at the sight: these are the Timberbottom Skulls, so called because they are from Timberbottom Far, Bradshaw. Their link to a haunting goes back 150 years.

The stories from that time include odd happenings when the skulls were disturbed: footsteps and strange noises would occur, and there was one

report from the family at the farm that they thought one night that something or someone was searching the whole premises.

Are the skulls the remains of some seventeenth century robbers? That is one theory.

Torture ; an illustration from Foxe's Nook of Martyrs showing what could happen to recusants

Whatever the origins, the record shows that earlier owners of the farm tried to remove the threat in various ways. Colonel Henry Hardcastle owned the farm at one time, and his grandfather had tried to bury the skulls in the churchyard to try to stop the unnerving events at the farm. Yet somehow the skulls were dug up later and carefully placed on a Bible, hoping that such a position would allay fears and perhaps stop the unnatural events.

The farm is no longer there, but the skulls are still on the Bible when not on display at Turton. This story has many parallels across the world, stories in which objects linked to unnatural and suspicious deaths seem to carry a curse with them when moved.

HALL I' TH' WOOD
CAVALIER

This hall is near Bolton and is the birthplace of a very famous man, one of the creators of the Industrial Revolution, Samuel Crompton, of the famous 'Mule' In the late Elizabethan years it was expanded by Lawrence Brownlow but was then sold to Christopher Norris. In turn, his son Alexander inherited. Norris was one of the body of men who administered land formerly-owned by Royalists supporters, and so he had enemies.

One of Norris's most recalcitrant and very active enemies was a cavalier, someone who has continued a reign of terror from the other side of the grave, it seems. He is heard during the Christmas season – in the form of footsteps on the stairs. There may be something related to the fact that a whole section of the original building was demolished by Alexander Norris, and maybe the spirit is trying to access something that is not visible now, to the living.

The famous incumbent came along in the eighteenth century, when the hall was converted into apartments and the Cromptons moved in, living there until 1782. Since 1900 it has been owned by the Corporation.

MYSTERY FIGURE AT CHINGLE HALL

A few years ago, Phil Stephens spent the night at Chingle Hall with some friends. They wanted to raise money for charity. What happened may be related to the traditions of this famously haunted spot. There was a knowledgeable guide with the party, so stories were told that would have prepared guests for possible paranormal happenings - hence the doubt that will open up lines of scepticism.

Notes made by the party included a feeling that someone was standing next to one person; someone while walking in the back garden was 'grabbed around the waist' ; an unknown force was holding closed the toilet door, and footsteps were heard. Add to that a smell of incense and it is clear that all is not normal at Chingle Hall.

The Hall is near Preston; the known history starts with one Adam de Singleton around 1260, but its central place in Lancashire history is again related to the persecution of recusants, so it was a place of refuge and secret meetings. Green reported in the 1970s that Ann Strickland, the sister of the then owner's wife, had found a pre-Reformation 'praying cross' and when a fireplace was removed a hiding place was found. Other details included drawers hidden in beams - places used to hide items and ornaments of Catholic worship. There is also a priest's room and that would have been used as a chapel.

The room considered haunted is known as the place where a monk's ghost is seen; the man who owned it when Green investigated, a Mr Howarth, said that he had seen this figure cross the small stone bridge and enter the house, then walk upstairs. Who is the figure? One theory is that he was John Wall, a man beheaded at Worcester in 1679 and whose head was taken to France by nuns. It was later brought back, and it may be that the head is buried somewhere in the Hall.

Andrew Green reported that a visitor in 1967 heard footsteps and other people heard footsteps a year later and they also reported a strange light. Maybe the events heard by Phil Stephens and friends are easily related to earlier stories. Chingle Hall has certainly been a target of ghost hunters in recent years and reports do come together convincingly. It is to be hoped that future investigators do not take guides with them, or if they do, then known stories are best told after the vigil, for obvious reasons.

More recently, Darren Ritson, in his book, Supernatural North, has reported: ' During my many days and nights at Chingle Hall I managed to experience and capture an array of paranormal activity including many anomalous sound recordings. One on occasion, while carrying out a séance in the great hall area we all heard the sounds of coins bouncing off the metal fire that stands in the room.'

The epic saga of Chingle Hall goes on.

HESKIN HALL

As several stories have already mentioned, Lancashire at the time of the religious dissensions in this land was a stronghold of Catholicism. Of all the tales of the depredations and savagery involved in these conflicts, few can equal the history of Heskin Hall, near Chorley.

When parliamentarian troops took the Hall a priest was found there and of course, his fate was sealed. But the captive tried to save his neck by betraying the family at the Hall and even offering to kill one of them himself to prove his loyalty to the parliament. He did so, but he was himself still hanged.

With such violent deaths linked to the place, it should be expected that there would be unexplained happenings there, and reports have been given of the little girl the priest hanged, usually seen in the scarlet bedroom. It is a very old place, records going back to 1212 when it was a Knight's fee, but it was bought by Richard Molyneux in 1556 and stayed in that family until 1739. After that it was owned by the Kershaws.

The ghost traditions are hearsay and local lore, but it is on record as being a place where religious martyrs were hanged. As for the uneasy and disturbing atmosphere, all we do know is that Lady Lilford, who lived here in the 1960's has described that her guests generally wished to leave the place in a hurry for some reason.

INCE HALL

Now a commercial office, Ince Hall has a long and eventful history. Writing in 1911, William Farrar and J. Brownbill wrote of it: 'The manor of Ince appears to have been a member of the royal manor of Newton before the Conquest... Richard de Ince occurs as late as 1333... the manor descended to Thomas Gerard of Ince who had a dispute with Sir Thomas Gerrard of Brynn, as to the possession of Turneshea Moss on the boundary of Ince and Ashton..' That hints at one feature of the history – opposition and enmity.

They also wrote at that time that 'The house now known as Ince Hall... near Rose Bridge, was originally surrounded by a moat. It was a good specimen of timber and plaster being erected in the reign of James I with a picturesque black and white front of five gables.' Coal pits were made there around 1880 and the writers lamented the loss of what could have been 'picturesque.'

So much for the place and its history. What about its haunting? One account of a visit there, around 180, says it all, in relation to a drawing he found:

' I examined it again and again, but not a single corner betrayed symptoms of lesion; it stuck bolt upright; and the dun, squat figures portrayed on it appeared to leer at me most provokingly.. I have always thought that the strong and eager impulse I felt for the possession of this hideous daub proceeded from a far different source than mere memorials of fondness for childhood...'

The writer's uncle, on being told about the frightening place and the bizarre and unearthly drawing, admitted that it might be haunted, adding, 'The foolish farmer and his wife who left did hint at something ghostly, but it is well known that I pay no attention to those tales...'

Now, there is little left to suggest that Ince Hall was once a place where visitors went with trepidation, but the investigations continue and anything may happen there. The very atmosphere invites a visit with an open mind.

Ince Hall also has the story of the dead hand. This concerns one of the owners of the hall in the earliest period, who was on his death bed and wanted to make a will. The lawyer came but was too late, but he was wrong, thinking that there was a little life left in the man, and he sent for a the dead hand kept at Bryn Hall. The belief was that rubbing the corpse with the dead hand would revive a dying man, and so that happened: the dead hand signed the will.

The funeral took place, but then trouble started when the man's daughter brought out what she thought was the valid will - one that left the property to herself and her brother. But the lawyer produced the will with the dead hand signature, and that will left everything to him. There was a fight to the death, and the lawyer was killed; a hex was on the place, because the son left the country, thinking he had killed the lawyer, but the crook recovered and tradition says that he killed the daughter so he could keep the land.

For centuries after, the ghost of a young woman was reckoned to be hanging in the air by the corrupt and murderous lawyer all his life, and she haunted a particular room in the hall. In more recent times, a gardener digging nearby found a skull, and it was that of a young women - it seems that she really was killed by the lawyer.

What about the dead hand? It has been said that this belonged to Father Edmund Arrowsmith, a Jesuit priest who had been executed at Lancaster in 1628, and he was seen as a martyr. The story is that his friends took his body, and they knew that he had asked them to cut off his hand, so it might work miracle cures on people in time to come. The hand was kept at Bryn Hall for a long time and then was taken to Garswood Hall, before a priest in the Catholic chapel at Ashton-in-Makersfield placed it there for curative purposes. In fact, in 1872 a woman called Catherine Collins came out of Salford Workhouse to walk to the chapel and have the touch of the dead hand. She was found exhausted on a doorstep in Wigan. The poor woman was prepared to walk all that way, as best she could, because she was partially paralysed on one side of her body. She could only walk very slowly, but such was her faith in the Dead Hand that she tried to get to the chapel. It

seems she never made it, as she had to be back in the workhouse before she could reach her destination.

Ince Hall An image from the nineteenth century print

SPIRITS EVERYWHERE AT MAINS HALL

There are lots of historical biographies linked to Mains Hall near Blackpool, not least the links to activities in priest holes. Writing in mid nineteenth century, the Rev Thurber related the first experience: ' From this hall-part was entered the pantry...with various coloured small stones... Here also when the workmen were pulling it down was disclosed a priest hole, between a stack of chimneys, which had been entered from a small upper closet, by a ladder; a most uncomfortable cell, both dark and confined, where the wretched inmate, Dr Allen, Father Campion and the persecuted priest of Titus Oates, in succession, stretched his limbs on the straw that was still found littering the straw.'

Thurber cannot resist imagining the painful past of the persecuted Catholics, and his words prefigure some more recent experiences there: ' Take heed how you tread on the time-worn boards. Since my last visit in 1845, it has been denuded of its interesting relics; even then desolation was triumphant. The picture of the Virgin and her infant son had fallen from its position over the altar...They were dead who had worshipped there...'

Of all the hounded people who sought sanctuary in the dark hole, there was a cardinal - Allen. It was said of him that even as he was hiding at Mains, he still spread tracts around the area which were dangerously subversive and would cost him his life if discovered. He wanted the Spanish Armada to land near Lancaster, and an old rhyme about this, using the word 'Norway' – the surname of King Philip – referring to an invasion:

'Between Boston's bay

And the Pile of Foudray,

Shall be seen the black navy of Norway.'

All this fear, apprehension and imminent insurrection exists in the history of the hall. But what of recent experience? Radio Lancashire devoted some time to a group exploration recently, and Janet Baron reported for the Where I Live web site. She recalled going into the priest hole, and then, she realised 'that we were entering a corridor with a horrible scary feel with spots of icy cold air.' Upstairs, Janet and her party experienced a strange light and noted that a door was somehow a cause of disquiet, and she learned that it had been used previously to lay out the dead. Finally, at the very top, the group were in darkness and Janet noted: ' Carole, myself and another member felt the floor moving... The cameras... would neither focus nor move properly.

Perhaps the most frequent sightings there have been of monks, as it has been said that twelve monks have been buried there. But there has been a claim by one writer that she made up the story when she was young and the 'urban myth' has spread. There were other responses to the report also, including one memory by a correspondent who wrote that when his parents once stayed at the Hall, they were woken up by the sound of a child crying in the bedroom. Some say that manifestations of children may originate in the children of the Hesketh family, some of whom died young, of one of the many killer diseases of Renaissance times. There have also been sightings, by several people, of a woman who stands at the top of the stairs. She had been given the name Lily, and the interesting side to this story is that the figure walks to stare as if out of a window, where there is no window, but as the web site information adds: 'Whilst renovating the old hall recently we found, behind modern plasterboard, an old original window in exactly the same location she seems to look out of..'

Whatever the truth is about who or what lies at Mains Hall, the history there, of people desperate to evade capture and fearing for their heads, is palpable. Over the years, historians and antiquarians have kept up an interest in the place, and its history is so rich that one always expects something new to be found there – and it might not be alive and in this dimension of time.

INVESTIGATION AT CHETHAM'S

C hetham's Hospital stands at the place where the earliest settlements in Manchester are found; there was formerly a baronial hall there and in 1421 the hall was changed to accommodate the staff for a new collegiate church. The religious college there somehow escaped the purges and damages of the reign of Henry VIII and then, in the Civil War, it was taken by Parliamentary forces.

The hospital and library have a long and distinguished history. Writing in 1929, the then Headmaster, W J Fielden, noted: ' Upwards of 4,150 boys have been placed on its foundation. The governors easily find places in the business houses for the boys – to have been educated at Chetham's Hospital being a great recommendation.'

In 2009 there was a paranormal investigation there by a team, led by a historian and some paranormal experts. They used a high level of technical equipment and made a thorough report. Around the bay window, people picked up the name 'Thomas' and bangs were heard by several of those present. There was a guest medium with the party, and the report noted: ' A nasty lady was felt in the room, she never had time for the children who stayed and learned there... she was the wicked step-mother type of person.' A spirit drawing was done as well during the stay. Later, a loud scream was heard and a shard of plastic fell from somewhere above. Phenomena were sensed in every room, and so the conclusions are vague, with no dominant figure lingering as the presence other reports might locate and feature.

LYDIATE

Lydiate Hall stands between the Mersey and the Ribble: close by are the remains of the abbey, constructed by Lawrence and Katherine Ireland at the end of the fifteenth century. The hall was apparently once surrounded by a moat, and by the gate house there was a mounting block, but in the interior there has been much of architectural interest. But in Victorian times, the interest was not concerned foremost with the buildings and carvings: it was the unexplained activity in the great parlour and 'squirrel chamber.' There were accounts of a man carrying a sword walking slowly through the rooms, then turning to look upwards, as if in prayer perhaps. In addition, there have been stories of a woman weeping coming from a corner of the Squirrel chamber.

Some explanations of the is that the figure is that of John de Lydiate, who was sent to Ireland by Edward II in 1325 to work in gathering provisions for the army of occupation. There is a possibility that the woman's cries and sighs are the ghost of Katherine Benetsone, a poor woman, who, after two marriages, was subject to an inquisition at Ormskirk, at which she was declared to be 'of unsound mind.'

At Lydiate Abbey, the haunting has apparently been of shrieking babies. In 1860, the abbey, or domestic chapel, was described by one historian: ' The ruins consist of the nave and the western tower.. the architecture is of a florid style.. and it is not easy to understand why the restoration of this little

A plan of Lydiate Hall showing the moat and gatehouse

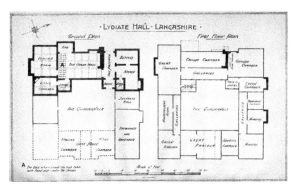

chapel was not undertaken as a place of worship for the Roman Catholics of the district...'

The source of the reported crying children is not sure, but the general commentary suggests that there were small children sacrificed here during the reign of Henry VIII. Of course, verification of these tales is always a challenge.

HAIGH HALL

Haigh Hall is about a mile and a half north east of Wigan. Earlier in history, it was the ancestral home of the Lindsay family, the Earls of Crawford and Balcarres. The Hall we see today was built much later, though, between 1827 and 1840. It is now part of Wigan Corporation.

The Hall, near Wigan, has a high reputation for things unnatural and unexplained. Staff there have reported several phenomena, such as this memory: ' Often, when I was heading towards the gate to go home, I'd automatically turn around because I could feel something there. It felt like I was leaving something behind.'

As with all old places with these atmospheres, we have to start with some history, and this has a story of a haunting attached. This is about Lady Mabel who married William Bradshaw in 1295. She was left at home when her husband went away to be a Crusader, and he was away for so long that she married again, this time to Henry Tudor. But Bradshaw was not dead. He came home and of course he was angry. In fact, Tudor was terrified and ran away, but Bradshaw collared him and killed him at Newbury Willows.

Not only is this a legend, but it is also the source of one of the novels by the great writer, Sir Walter Scott. His novel, The Betrothed, although he transposed matters to a different setting. The last Bradshaw died in 1787 and the Haigh property was inherited by Elizabeth Dalrymple.

The Betrothed: a picture from a 1926 edition of Sir Walter Scott's novel

Of course, poor Mabel had committed bigamy and had to do a penance; she had to walk barefoot while carrying a candle from the Hall to where she could see a church. That means she would stop at Mab's Cross. It may seem markedly strange, but workers have reported her ghost walking with the candle and tiny footprints have been found.

In the parkland around the Hall there is a place called Monkshill, and even that is a place where a ghost has been seen- a forester claims he saw a figure floating above the ground. One of the workers has said that he had heard weird things happen:'You hear a lot of banging upstairs when you know there isn't anybody up there. A while ago, I went upstairs to lock the doors and walked past one of the rooms. It sounded like someone was rummaging around, but we knew there wasn't anyone in there.'

CLAYTON HALL
POLTERGEIST

Clayton Hall, on Ashton New Road, Manchester, is now a grade II listed building, dating back to the fifteenth century. After ownership by various members of the Clayton family, it passed into the hands of the Byrons (of Lord Byron fame) and then by Chethams. Eventually, it was bought by Manchester City Corporation. To look at it now, there is no suggestion of the disturbing poltergeist reported there. The overall chronicle of the hall includes three ghost stories, but the poltergeist that has been known to make a mess of bed sheets, create irritating noises on stairs and push people over - usually servants - tends to take centre stage.

It appears that the time in the past most likely to have had violent deaths around the place is one again the Civil War. The Royalist army was focused on the hall before the attack on the city, and at that time Cromwell himself stayed there after the fight. Lines of thought non this suggest that there was once again blood on his hands, and that the ghostly presence was one of his men's victims. It is amazing just how many tales of this kind relate to the Civil War, and Lancashire has most of them. Although the story of Bolling Hall in Bradford equals the best, with a heart-rending story of the spirit appealing to the general in charge to 'Pity poor Bradford.'

There is also nearby Dunkenhalgh Hall, once owned by the Walmesley family and later by the French family, the Petres. The story there is that a governess of the Petres, one Lucette, fell in love with a visitor to the hall back in the eighteenth century. It's a case of unrequited love and the poor girl took her own life by hurling herself into the river Hyndburn. Her ghost has reportedly been seen in a shroud of white, around the hall.

WYCOLLER HALL

This is a place with resonances in all kids of contexts, even having Bronte connections. Wycoller was built in the early sixteenth century, coming into the hands of the Cunliffe family in the early 1600s. The story of the house is one of those tales in which horrible murder and a haunting go hand in hand, because in the 1660s the wife of Simon Cunliffe, although 'murder' is not really the right word. This is because the events leading to the death were frightening, but the death perhaps not intended: Simon led a hunt for a fox one day and the animal ran into the hall and into the wife's room, and the men pursued. Simon rode his horse upstairs and foolishly took his whip, as he thought it was disgusting that his wife was so terrified. In that action, she died of fright.

The ghost seen at the hall is alleged to be that of the cruel husband, still walking the place where his stupidity caused his wife's death. It is said that you can hear the sound of his horse on the nearby bride and on the stairs sometimes. Some say that this happens only once a year. Of course, one would expect the victim to appear also, and two lovers once reported that they had seen her shade, wearing a black silk dress. She was seen also by some workmen. It is said that , as one old account has it, ' When the wind howls the loudest, the spectral horseman comes... he makes his way up the broad oak staircase... dreadful screams are then heard from a woman which gradually subside into groans. The horseman then makes his appearance at the door, at once mounts his horse and gallops away, the way he came.'

The man's poor victim is reckoned to have foretold the ruin of the family before she died, and of course, eventually this was to be true.

The place certainly has character and atmosphere; it is almost verified that Charlotte Bronte used the hall as the fictional Ferndean Manor in Jane Eyre. Howarth is not far away, and the Brontes did visit the Cunliffe family. Other hints exist too, such as the fact that Elizabeth Cunliffe became Elizabeth Eyre when she married, and there are some similarities between Mr Rochester and Henry Owen Cunliffe.

Perhaps also of great interest to Bronte enthusiasts is the fact that a Cunliffe married a West Indian woman, but supposedly threw his wife overboard on the return journey. In Jane Eyre, the Rochester connection with the Caribbean Masons of a major part of the plot, but of course Rochester does not kill his poor mad wife: he simply locks her up in an attic room and pretends she does not exist.

GAWTHORPE HALL

This beautiful and elegant building is close to Padiham, and is a wonderful example of Elizabethan architecture, created in 1600. Once again, Charlotte Bronte figures in the history here: she was a friend of the Kay-Shuttleworth family who owned the house through all its history up to that point in the mid nineteenth century. The house was redesigned at the time Charlotte went there, by Sir Charles Barry. Charlotte went there twice; on the first occasion it was in response to Kay-Shuttleworth's intense need to meet and talk to the author 'Currer Bell' - Charlotte's pen name. The second time was more prosaic, because it was a job interview for her husband, the rev Arthur Bell Nicholls, for a potential living at Haberhalgh.

Before the Most Haunted team went there for an investigation, it had always been said that the last Kay-Shuttleworth, Rachel, haunted the building, and there has always been the theory that another Shuttleworth, involve din the Pendle witch trials, also haunted the place. All manner of phenomena were seen and heard by the television team: the chandelier in the hall swung around; crayons and paper were left in the nursery and later, images had been drawn on the paper, and the crew reported that crayons had been thrown at them.

In the servants' quarters, Yvette Fielding reported that her name was called. Staff at the hall had over the years talked about what they had seen and heard so some things were confirmed by the television visit. Most dramatic was this comment:

'We also spotted what seemed to be a group of people on our thermal imaging camera, stood looking down on the crew from the landing but only our crew were in the body of the hall.' There was also a handed-down tale of a young woman being murdered there but there was no provenance given to that. What one really wants to know is a reason why Rachel Shuttleworth would want to haunt the hall.

Regarding Charlotte Bronte, her second visit was not long before she died. As Mrs Gaskell wrote: ' Soon after her return [from Gawthorpe] she was attacked by new sensations of perpetual nausea and ever-increasing faintness.' She died not long after that. It would come as no surprise to find that Gawthorpe had yet more tales to offer.

A CRIME AND A BRIDE

In 1868 a writer received an offer to stay in an old Lancashire mansion with some friends and admirers. He was in for an experience that would shock him to the bones. Even before he went, he had a picture in his mind about where he was going: ' I have a great love for these old mansions.. their many gables, with well carved barge-boards, their broken outlines and beautiful pargetting render them most picturesque...' All that suggests a pleasant little holiday. What a shame it didn't turn out that way.

The house overlooked Longridge Fell, and the writer recalled that 'The country around is somewhat bare...as to the house, the whole was surrounded by a moat which has been recently filled up.. the oldest part of the building is undoubtedly the large hall. There is a screen and a doorway, and above the hall a minstrel gallery.' He remained in a pleasant mood when he arrived and was greeted by the owner, saying 'A grand old place, and with a goodly history and a right pleasant thing it must be to picture it in imagination.' He went into a long description of the imagined history, thinking of the 'maidens' who had been 'swept in dance over the polished floor' and our genial writer even went into poetry:

'With love demure

And soul all pure

Thinking of her lover's words...'

He then asked the owner if there was a ghost story attached to the place, thinking it would be an amusing thing. The man relied,

' Why so there is... it is something about a crime and a bride, but we have never been able to learn any more than this. However, there is a haunted chamber...you may sleep in it.'

'By all means.. I may perhaps learn something more' the writer replied, still thinking this would merely be some fun.

After sitting in the library with a stomach nicely lined with food, the writer retired to bed. As he was dozing, he heard footsteps coming up the stairs and a figure walked into the room. It was a man, dressed as if for the hunt of for a scrap, and it was as if he had stepped out of the fifteenth century. The writer recalled:' the figure, leaning over my bed, said that there were curses flung at him before he and his friends were slaughtered and the thing moaned, 'Would that my bones could find sanctuary!'

The writer was slowly recovering some composure and said, 'of course, my friend will be delighted to... to oblige you. Do they lie near the hall, and to any great depth?'

The ghost did not speak, but gave three solemn knocks, and then cried as it faded.

The writer jumped out of bed, and explained what happened next:

' *In the corner where the ghost had first appeared I noticed a glass door,*
Apparently communicating with an inner chamber and there was a quantity
Of white cloth over a clothe shores. I blushed to think what I had imagined.'

That seemed like an explanation, and the owner asked at breakfast if his guest had had a good sleep. He was feeling a fool as he answered yes. So that should have been the end of it.

But a month later, when builders were digging to repair a wall, they found three human skeletons.

CLEGG HALL

Clegg Hall was in former times, as one Victorian writer put it, 'infested with boggarts.'

This hall, near Rochdale, is supposed to be the site of a murder: an uncle killed two orphan children who were given to him to care for; they were also to be heirs to the estate, but he wanted that for himself. This was in very early times, and even though the house was rebuilt in 1620, the story still held that the boggarts tormented anyone who went within the walls. Eventually, there was an attempt to lay the ghosts, as an old account relates:

'A pious monk in the neighbourhood was long importuned to exorcise the ghosts and at last consented. Having provided himself with a number of charms and spells, he boldly called on them to appear and established connections with them.'

He regretted that. The sprites offered some domestic peace, but for a price. In fact, they asked for a sacrifice of a body and a soul. The old tale goes that the monks agreed, and the local crowd who had gathered with him shivered in fear and some ran to hide where they could. But the canny old monk gave the boggarts the body of a cock and the sole of a shoe. The boggarts left. It's good to have some humour in one of these tales from the ancient buildings; it takes away some of the staleness of some records, and smacks of a little genuine oral history.

ELIZABETH STILL WAITS – RUFFORD OLD HALL

Rufford Old Hall is a beautiful building, built in 1530 by Sir Thomas Hesketh at Penwortham. It has the possibly amazing footnote in its history that Shakespeare may have performed there, because a certain 'William Shakeshaft' is recorded as being in the Hesketh company of players in 1585. In 1661 it was extended when a new wing was built and then again in 1820 still more was added. It was owned by Hesketh family until 1936 when it was acquired by the National Trust.

Not surprisingly, its ghost relates to the Hesketh story.

There are allegedly two spirits present: one is the White Lady – a young woman in her wedding dress said to be Elizabeth Hesketh whose husband had died in battle, yet she still waits for him to come home. She was told that the fight was over and that her groom would be coming home, so she set about making plans for the wedding. The day of the wedding came and she put on her dress, praying that he would soon be back at her door.

But then came the fateful messenger with the real news – as sad as could be expected. He was dead. Her ghost waits by the window, still looking for him, hoping that the news was not true.

There have been sightings of a male ghost too: one was of such a figure floating over the canal nearby, and another of a man in Elizabethan clothes in the great hall. The Most Haunted team were there in 2010 and they found activity in the nursery and in the hall. The medium claimed to have the information that Robert Hesketh, who inherited the estate in the sixteenth century, had been possessed by an 'evil spirit' which had eaten him up in an agonising way before he finally died of black jaundice. One story they had which so far has no historical basis is of a woman killed where the west wing now is, and Yvette Fielding had a vision of being in a topiary garden – which in fact is where the west wing was placed in earlier times.

Part II

ORDINARY AND EXTRAORDINARY TALES

This section is concerned with a mixed bag of paranormal experiences from a range of places and situations. Mostly, the locations are very ordinary. Most of these tales have no dimension suggesting the words 'legend' or 'traditional tale'. Some of these are embedded in historical documentation while others relate purely to tradition and oral history. I have used many of these from previous investigations, and so there is a subjective element present, but the writers are mostly well known as careful investigators. One thing here stands out – the nature of place. We used the word 'location' rather easily in paranormal studies, but in fact, one of the most fascinating ongoing debates in this area of work is the way in which places can retain energies from the past: the possibility that some kind of absorption is at work where there has been a strong, emotional human tie to the place for some reason. It may not in all cases be suffering that is the tie. In some cases it is a pleasant association, but the point is that extreme emotion of some kind is the common factor.

Still, we also have here the extraordinary as well, and I have included a famous ballad. Sometimes, on rare occasions to be sure, a piece of ancient writing does have a tenuous link to something observed in recent times.

THE SWINTON GHOST

Peter Hough told this tale of the Bull's Head in Swinton, relating to events in 1985. It started with a staff discussion of the supposed haunting taking place at the pub, and everything seemed to suggest a poltergeist; it was decided that the party would settle down for the night, on the floor, and see what happened. There was a faint air of scepticism and light-heartedness, but that vanished when, as Peter relates, lights flashed, beer barrels started rolling around and one man heard what he described as a swishing of a broom right next to him.

But this was far from a harmless jape, a little messing around with spirits. One man was gashed severely and had to be taken to Hope Hospital to have stitches over his eye. The report after the event was that the man in question 'Was full of life, always telling jokes, but his experience has changed him.'

It comes as no surprise to learn that the Bull's Head has a long history: it was first built in the sixteenth century but reached its modern form in 1826. One element of social history that appeals to the researcher is that it was close to a graveyard and that men used to keep guard looking out for body snatchers in the days when grave robbers could earn good money stealing corpses for use by anatomists and medical students. Peter also points out that there is a bricked-up arch in the cellar. It is indeed a place of mystery.

Later investigations recorded that the family who bought the pub and lived there in 1985 had experienced strange happenings, such as a stool moving in an office and then also a clock jumping off the wall and smashing on the floor. There was also the business with the lights: on one occasion the pub was locked and lights were on, but as one family member walked across the landing, all lights went out, in sequence.

Peter Hough, writing in 1990, updated the chronicle of events: 'As I was writing this, I learned that a female member of [the landlady] had a frightening experience. It happened at 2 p.m. when the girl was at the bottom of the stairs ... she was about to ascend the stairs when she saw something gliding down them. It had a vague shape and outline like a monk. As it drew nearer, her consciousness faded...'

Thanks to Peter, we have a meticulous record of one set of poltergeist actions, and lots of secondary stories to match the first rather playful investigation on the fateful night when the group had the shock of their lives. His writings show that he is methodical and open-minded, and he even considered that the man hurt that night might have been trying a prank. It has to be agreed that such a thing was very unlikely indeed, given the seriousness of his injury.

POLTERGEIST IN ROCHDALE

The second case from Peter Hough concerns a family who lived in a bungalow in Rochdale. The beginning of the investigation was a chance reading of a news item saying that the family had a drip from the ceiling and that no council work or study could explain it. Peter was chairman of the Northern Anomalies Research Organisation at the time and he decided on an investigation. A damp patch on a wall had started to seep water and no known origin was found. But the water could spring up elsewhere as well.

After several attempts to combat and understand a series of water-related occurrences, there was a new development: the couple watched a door handle turn and a door open, but no-one was present, and then there was an unexplained smell of tobacco. Things began to get decidedly worse then: coughing sounds in the corner, and then water from close to a light-fitting. Then one person became wet even when she had not been near water.

Peter Hough had to consider the possibility that he was dealing with a poltergeist. As he wrote of two possible scenarios: ' In the mundane scenario the subject deliberately creates phenomena in order to attract attention... In the paranormal scenario phenomena are produced as a direct consequence of negative emotional energy unwittingly crated by the focus.' He decided on a team investigation. Incidents were recorded – numerous and baffling. For instance, a man's voice was heard, a statuette was moved and in the hallway there was a fragrant smell of hyacinths.

As matters turned out, there was an instance of trickery detected, but Peter still concluded that one instance did not invalidate the case. Was one observed deliberate action something that would negate all other details observed? Not at all, although questions would have to be asked.

CHEETHAM AND SHUDEHILL TALES

In 1964 there were strange occurrences in an ordinary house in Cheetham, and all the signs were of a poltergeist: a dressing table moved of its own volition, there were whistles and cries, and a black figure was seen.

Perhaps a planchette was the wrong move here, because that is what the family did, and the results were horrific, with the words of a supposed man beyond the grave talking about a murdered child. The information gained in the activity prompted the family to search the house and they found old papers were found, along with two items most disturbingly linked to the subject of the planchette interaction: first a music score which conveyed music close to the whistled melodies they had heard, and then small bones found underneath the floorboards.

Those two findings would seem to support the ghostly communication, but in fact the bones found were those of a rabbit.

Also around Manchester, as Peter Underwood has reported, an antiques shop in Shudehill was the scene of a haunting – this time by a Jacobite ghost. The man who was troubled by the spectre described it as having red hair and carrying a dagger. The man who told Underwood the tale said that the figure seemed to stare at a Jacobite painting on the wall, and the

This is very ordinary school scene suggests nothing disturbing and uneasy, but the history is very different.

theory was that the ghost was James Stewart, a man who came south with Bonnie Prince Charlie's army. There were also other reports of unnatural events in the house, such as one occasion when a loud crashing noise from the cellar was heard when no-one was down there.

A SOUTHPORT STORY

Peter Underwood, in his collection of stories published in 1971, provides our first story in this collection from Southport. This story concerns the Palace Hotel, and things started to happen during demolition. The Electricity Board investigated when workmen reported noises and voices from empty rooms: nothing was found to suggest that any power was going into the premises. Groups of men saw doors open and shut: so stories were corroborated.

As one person came to visit the workers, she saw a lift move but without sound. When the men and the visitor went to look at the lift they found the brake on, so how could the lift have moved? Even with cables cut, the lift would not move, so how had it been raised to the second floor? The focus of paranormal activity was almost certainly a spot on the second floor, and Underwood adds to that line of thought when he notes that a dog was shown on film, stopping at the spot on the second floor, and standing stationary, refusing to walk on past the apparently highly charged place.

The story supports the view that places where something deeply traumatic has happened can be subject to energies we do not yet understand. The familiar experience of one's hairs standing on end and seeing things from the corner of the eye may well related to the kind of sixth sense perceptions animals seem to have for the response to such phenomena.

THE POLICEMAN'S
PRESENCE

L iverpool was one of the most hard-hit cities in the Blitz of World War II. In Liverpool there were eighty raids between August 1940 and June, 1942. The peak was the period of a full week of continuous bombing that took place in May, 1941. The city was a primary target for the Nazis, as it was the centre of importation from America; night attacks were launched, and planes approached the Mersey from the Welsh coastline, and pilots would have seen the lights of Dublin to the west, and so been able to determine their location.

In the thousands of casualties of the bombs there was a police officer who was not only popular but he had distinctive habits, including tapping a railing with his truncheon, and although he died in the war, his ghost was seen in 1971 when people in one area where he walked his beat reported seeing his figure walking and tapping the truncheon. So accurate were the descriptions that it was all very convincing; one man even noted the figure had a tin hat and carried a bag – both items traceable to the habits of police in the war years. This appears to back up the theory that many apparitions relate to the familiar routine movements of the person in life, just as people are seen on roads or doing jobs they did a thousand times when alive. Certainly, a police beat is something of a loop, and so if time intersects, as some theorise, then there is more chance of such phenomena in locatiosn where repeated routine movement has occurred.

PEEL HALL SPECTRE

Andrew Green's case book from the 1970s gives us this report of an apparition at Astley Green. This relates to an old farm building which was for some time the focus of countless tales of weird happenings. Green recalls that a former policeman went to stay overnight there to get closer to the truth of the stories.

These tales included a vision of a lady in white and paintings being dragged from the wall. There was also a second sighting, by a boy, of a white figure floating in the trees around the farm. The usual explanations were offered: the woman in white was a murder victim, and so the interpretation was spread and believed. But there was no mention of any research or supporting information in that regard. Only rarely do paranormal investigations looking at local lore and oral tradition follow up in the archives of crime. It was therefore up to the ex-policeman to see and report things.

Unfortunately, he left and reported nothing of any interest.

PRISONER'S GHOST

Given that a prison cell or a dungeon represent the worst misery imaginable for some of the poor wretches shoved into these enclosed tombs over the worst time sin history, there should be more paranormal prisoner tales, but there are not so many in circulation. However, there is one dour and grim tale from the Stork Hotel at Billinge.

The hotel was used as a prison by Cromwell (how often does he crop up in these tales?) in 1640. Down in the cellars, one poor victim was cast into darkness to be abandoned and he eventually died down there. If the man is the resident spirit - and some have seen glasses move and heard footsteps on the floor above - then he is in a convivial place and in good fellowship. The only problem is that he is from the shadow world and the other inhabitants just want a quiet drink and a chat with other living souls.

It has been said that the ghost of the prisoner has been known to walk over the sleeping bodies of those staying at the place.

If we were to expect paranormal experiences in Lancashire in relation to places of battle and conflict, there are dozens of locations linked to the Civil War. One place whence reports should emanate is surely the A49 along Wigan Lane, for instance, because there, in 1651 the Earl of Derby's met the parliamentarians under Robert Lilburne, whose met resisted a fierce attack and stayed in the hedgerow. The Royalists gave in and scattered. Any sightings from what has become known as the Battle of Wigan Lane will be welcome to investigators. Meanwhile the tales of prisoners and executed men dominate the traditional tales.

FEAR IN SACKVILLE STREET

There is something about the phenomenon of an apparition or a poltergeist that seems to attract their activity towards joyful, gregarious occasions, and they appear, like the spirit of Banquo at Macbeth's dinner, on many occasions, to tell us something important or at least to make us act - often to run away and never go back to the place.

There was once a house-warming party in Sackville Street, Everton, and the occasion was memorable to all who were present - but for the wrong reasons. The woman and her family moved into the house and the party was arranged. Then, in the midst of all the jollification, there was something amiss - sounds from upstairs when there was quite patently no-one up there. The first person heard some footsteps, all went quiet and then everyone heard them.

The whole group went up to look around the attics but nothing was found that could be interpreted as being the possible cause of the disturbance. A decision was made, so convinced was the party that there was someone hiding upstairs, that the police should be called, and some men set off to bring an officer or at least report the noise. Two men then went upstairs again for another look. What happened next was a complete shock to everyone.

As one man was coming back downstairs, he felt as if someone or something was lifting him up, after taking hold of him around his waist. He later said that he 'seemed to be wafted down'.

The house-warming was not the end of the fearful events, not by a long way. For several nights afterwards, there were more noises upstairs and it became unbearable. They were only tenants, and so it was an easy decision to move out and admit defeat. All the furniture was going to be moved to the ground floor in preparation for that. The men went to do that, followed by one of the women. Reports later said that she was seen to be wafted into the air and held in suspension for some time, and then she was lowered, as if on a current of air. Witnesses said that she screamed and that there was some bright light around her.

The poor woman went through a doorway to another room and there she was found, out cold. She was, of course, taken to hospital. The source of the terror was never found nor explained.

THE PHANTOM VOICE

Two hundred years ago, the coast around Southport, as one commentator at the time wrote, was a place of sandbanks and therefore of shipwrecks, and often these wrecks happened at night; the place where people went to enjoy the sea-bathing and fresh air was also a perilous place for seamen.

One memory, from the Regency years, is a story by a man on horseback who ventured into this area at night. His story begins with his sense of isolation:' It was a feeling of loneliness, of dread, that seemed to haunt me... The demon of fear seemed to possess my frame and benumbed every faculty. I saw, or thought I saw, shapes hideous but indistinct rising before me...'

He sensed a rustling noise close to his ear, but went on. Then his horse stopped suddenly and would not move. Before him was the sad and mystical moaning of the sea. He decided to walk on very slowly but the horse would not budge. Then, as he concentrated on listening to what sounds were around him, he thought he heard a voice in the distance. Soon some words being shouted became clearer: someone was yelling 'Murder... murder!' He bravely walked towards the sound of the voice, in a mist, with chill air all around him. The horse then made a dreadful sound, tugged away from him and bolted.

The poor traveller then made out a figure on the ground some short distance ahead, and he quickened his pace. Close, in the poor light of the moon, he saw a human shape and a hand was rising towards him. He took hold of it, thinking it was someone in dire need of help, when he winced with fear. The man was sure that he had grasped the hand of a corpse. The poor traveller recalled falling into a swoon after that, before coming to consciousness and then wanting to run from the place, of course.

He described how he dashed from the place then: 'fear then prompted me to flee... the moon now enabled me to follow a beaten track.' Eventually, he sat down, shivering, and when he gathered himself a little he realised that there was a light not far away. It was a tavern. But he was not sure what had happened, He remembered passing out after touching the hand. The secret was kept to himself until some time later when he wrote it all down.

TERRIFYING TERRACES

Derelict buildings have an aura of mystery and menace, and many paranormal narratives emanate from them. This is one such typical account.

Some reports of paranormal stories seem to circulate in hearsay and urban myths. Often there is an item on the internet and then a paranormal investigation group takes up a challenge after a reconnaissance of the location. This appears to have happened with a line of deserted terraces in north Manchester. Sightings have included an old lady looking out from a window and a rag and bone man, with his cries being heard as he trots his cart around the area. The principal source is apparently a person who moved into the terrace in the 1930s and since the place became derelict figures have been seen and heard down by a stretch of water close to the houses.

This, and other narrative elements, were put together by investigator Leigh G Banks recently and he conveys the tale in semi-fictional form, so it is hard to see where the roots of the phenomena lie. Banks uses high empathic imagination to recreate the story, so it is not clear what the sources are.

The one element that persists, though, is the face at the window – probably the woman from the 1930s. As with so many hauntings in domestic settings, there is a tragic story behind the image; from that era, the suffering is obvious – poverty, hard work and deprivation, in the days before the welfare state. Yet whatever the sources, the fact is that at any time the face might be there, looking on, either seeing us today, or still looking on the world there as it was eighty years ago.

A similar case was reported from Rochdale in the 1970s and in that 'face at the window' tale many thought they saw the face of a man who had been a local farmer, and who had killed himself after his business failed.

RADCLIFFE LEGEND

This county story hooks into the body of ballad literature, so significant is the tragic tale behind it: it has come down in a ballad version called 'Lady Isabella's Tragedy', and it also relates to the universal traditions of the 'black dog' or guytrash as well, but the main narrative concerns, as the sub-title to the ballad has it: ' The step-mother's cruelty, being the story of a lamentable and cruel murder committed on Lady Isabella, the only daughter of a noble duke...'

Radcliffe Tower was built in the reign of Henry IV by James Radcliffe, a man who married a daughter of William Tempest of York. It is now a scheduled monument. The ballad tale is clearly a legend - one relating to common stories of cannibalism in the folk literature, and used by Shakespeare in Titus Andronicus, of a man eating his child's carcass unknowingly. In the balled, the daughter of the noble man is killed and baked in a pie, then we have this stanza:

Oh then bespake the scullion boy
With a lid voice so high-
If you will now your daughter see,
My Lord, cut up that pie....

The tale is grossly told, dealing with the most repulsive aspects of such tales, as it ends with this, as the Lord takes revenge:

'Likewise he judged the master-cook

In boiling lead to stand;

And made the simple scullion boy

The heir to all his land.'

The key question is: the sightings of a ghostly black dog at the site - are such things the spirits of the murdered person? It's a wild thought. But then we know nothing substantial about black dog appearances. One of the most extensive accounts of black dog appearances - creatures called by various names including gytrash, shuck and bargest - is by Alastair MacGregor who has summarised possible lines of thought about them as being that they are incarnations of the Devil, portents of death or that they appear at a location where there has been a notable atrocity. It seems a long stretch of imagination to link a black dog appearance to the old ballad, though.

Writing in 1950, MacGregor wrote about the black dog in the northern counties: ' Some of the dogs are said to be headless... at Endmoor it has been lately seen, running by a wall.. In the north, they are regarded as apparitions or death, "If a black dog follows after you, comes near you, and won't run away, said some in Furness recently, it is a sure sign of death,Äù. ' He found dozens of similar stories throughout Lancashire and Westmorland, as it then was.

All this is difficult to link to the horrific old ballad, but one thing is for sure - Radcliffe Tower is, and has been for some time, peculiarly

This old print shows the eerily atmospheric place, even in ruins.

atmospheric, a place of past violence and trauma. It is one of those places tucked away from view, well overdue for a team to stage a proper paranormal investigation and a vigil there.

Coming down to earth, the Radcliffes of Ordsall are recorded more prosaically, in book of hours kept at the Bodleian Library. This once belonged to Elizabeth Atherton, sister to Sir William Radcliffe, and it was a treasured possession of the family. One feature of this of special interest is that it has a number of badges attached, including a 'badge of the five wounds' and even this is an array of disturbing images, including one of Christ showing his wounds to a monk. But the book lists dozens of Radcliffes throughout the Sixteenth Century, reminding us that there was a family of the name , and that not all connected with the remains is pure fantasy.

RINGLEY VICARAGE

Peter Underwood, in his autobiography, No Common Task, gives an account of strange happenings at Ringley Vicarage near Bolton, many years ago. He was writing in 1983 and went there because there had been reports that two inhabitants had left the place in a hurry for some reason. One vicar, the Rev. Butterworth, moved into the place and then objects moved, footsteps were heard and doors would shut of their own volition. Underwood said that there was such a terrible feeling inside the walls that an exorcism was effected, but things went from bad to worse. During the exorcism, the temperature of the room varied greatly and still the noises and movements continued.

It was the last straw for the vicar when someone visiting the home said they saw a frightening figure rather like a gargoyle; then his son was found with his mattress on top of him – a mattress that had been propped against a wall earlier in the day, and finally, before the vicar gave in and left the place forever, he saw the ghost of a woman, and she spoke, telling him that she was called Agnes. He was deeply shocked and took some time to gather himself t cope with what had happened – and clergymen are used to dealing with the dead, as it were.

Yet there was also another presence. The vicar before the Rev Butterworth had left in fear also, reporting a disturbing presence. It was ripe for investigation, and Underwood, a man vastly experienced in these matters and President of the famous Ghost Club, went with his wife, Joyce. He reported: ' We interviewed several people who were convinced that the place was haunted, and one who was certain that it was not! The place had, or has, a very curious atmosphere, but we decided there was insufficient good evidence to warrant a full-scale investigation.'

That kind of contrast- in which intelligent and education people give testimony to paranormal events and then the professionals find nothing conclusive – is a familiar pattern in these affairs. Underwood was always very thorough and had an open mind. He was always careful and methodical. His conclusions were probably wide and well considered. The problem is that two men of the cloth had seen and heard things beyond their explanation, and numerous visitors had corroborated these experiences.

What is of wider interest in this case is that of vicarages generally as haunted locations. There is no doubt that there may well be a link between the professional lives and beliefs of the incumbents and the supposed occurrences, and of course these buildings are often near graveyards. Underwood concludes, with these thoughts in mind, ' I don't think that there is any doubt that there are more haunted rectories and vicarages than any other type of inhabited building, and I have often wondered whether concentrated thought has anything to do with such haunted houses...'

THE VOICE IN THE CAR AND A VOICE IN HULME

This is a tale most of us would find deeply disturbing, and yet, it is one of those experiences in which the dead come back to help us, so the fear has a pleasant, good feeling - after the shock has passed.

The dead supposedly communicate directly to us when there are things of importance to be said or hinted at, or even apparitions occur in this way simply to let us know that the spirits are there, still, with us. There are countless experiences on record of the recently dead communicating by such means as touching the shoulder, tapping an arm or whispering. There is a pattern of such things in the period immediately after a funeral, it appears. In my own investigations, I have had at least a dozen tales of such things, often on stairways or while the person was moving, which again suggests a repeated pattern of behaviour.

Such a story was told by Graham Coates-Gibson on a paranormal web site. He drove his sister from Tyneside home to Bolton for their mother's funeral, and then drove home again. On that drive, something happened that all drivers dread: he was low on petrol and had forgotten to take his wallet with him.

He decided to drive on and cope with things when he finally had no choice but to stop, and he was on the M62 motorway, trying to drive so that he could economize on his use of his remaining fuel, when he heard a voice form behind- from the seat in which his mother had been used to sit in. The voice said, Keep going, twin... just keep going.' Grahame's mother called him Twin (he was a twin brother) and so he was convinced as to the origin of the words. Amazingly, the car kept going, even though there were another sixty miles to cover and the light on the dashboard told Graham he was running out of petrol.

This amazing 'everyday paranormal' tale ended when he reached home, pulled up in the drive, and heard the voice say 'Goodnight son' behind him. The garage told him that they had never seen a car so dry. The experience was totally convincing to him, and he added in his account of life with that car that on one occasion his daughter had said she couldn't sit in that same seat - she said there was someone already there.

As a coda to the story, I have a personal experience to add. After my father's death I was in our sitting-room at about the time he used to put on his uniform as a security officer working at a local university. He used to walk upstairs for his uniform at nine every evening when it was his shift. On that occasion, just a week after his funeral, I sensed a noise on the stairs, and I went upstairs to see what it was. On the way up, I felt a force rub against an arm.

When I recovered from the shock, I glanced at the clock in the upstairs lounge. It was a few minutes after nine.

Just a week after that I was in the kitchen reading the paper. I was looking at the racing pages; my father was a very keen racing fan and liked a flutter. As I looked down the race card I heard a whisper from the spot near the outside back door where he used to stand when cooking. It said ' Any one you like son...' It was the phrase he used when he asked me to pick horses and have a bet with him.

In the records, voices appear to be less common than touch, but both occur frequently soon after a passing into the shadow world of the spirits.

One of the classic examples of this, because it appeared in one of the formative books in paranormal studies, Phantasms of the Dead, is from Hulme. A Mrs Thompson from Boston Street reported her experience to the Society for Psychical Research. The event happened in 1873, and concerns her fiancé, who had gone back to his home in Yorkshire after paying a visit to Hulme, where he had made a silly bet with his lady, for some gloves. This is what happened, in the words of the correspondent:

'On December 18th I awoke in the night, hearing someone earnestly calling my name. I rose, and went down to my mother's room on the floor beneath and asked her if she knew who had called me... I went back to bed, feeling ill at ease... shortly afterwards I distinctly heard the voice calling me... I stayed with my mother the rest of the night. The next day we heard that Harry had suddenly died that night...'

CARLETON CREMATORIUM

In July, 1936, Carleton Crematorium near Blackpool was opened, and not long afterwards a taxi-driver from Layton told the local press that he had been terrified when going out there. He had seen what he was sure was a ghost of a green hue – he clearly saw the body and the face. According to local writer, Juliette Gregson, the original article noted that he had seen the ghost close to a murder location.

Near to Robins Lane a widow had been battered to death, and of course the theory that ghosts of murdered people are commonly seen or heard at the place of such a violent death.

The driver back in 1936 had a passenger: he collected a woman late at night at North Shore station and she wanted to go to Robin's Lane in Carleton; we can imagine the poor man's shock when, as he approached Robin's Lane, his passenger asked him to change direction – because the road led to the crematorium. It was almost midnight, in December, and he was about to drive to a dark place of death.

The man said that he stopped by the gates and his passenger was about to get the money to pay him, from her purse, when he looked outside and saw the face. He described it in these words: 'It was the face of an old man, with sunken eyes, long dark hair, a Punch-like nose and prominent chin.' The driver was surely more startled though, by the horrendous yell of fear from his back seat, as the woman saw the green face as well. At least someone had corroborated what he had seen, but she got out and ran away as if chased by the Devil and ran down the side of the crematorium.

The face and shape of the old man then moved to the front of the cab, and slowly faded away. Thoughtfully, as he guessed that the poor woman he had taken there was hiding in the bushes somewhere not too far away, he reversed and shone his headlights into the path where he had last seen her. But there was no-one there and no response.

Naturally, as his passenger had seen the phantom, when the driver told the local paper what had happened, there was an attempt to find the scared woman so that she could come forward and back up the tale. But she was never found. We can only speculate as to why she never came forward. But from the story it seems to be totally true that she really was there: her scream was real enough to make the driver's heart jump.

THE BLACK HEAD

O f all the tales collected here, this has to be one of the most bizarre, being not supernatural but equally strange. It originates from Chambers Journal in the nineteenth century and was reprinted in The Lancashire Gazette. The unknown author told the tale like an oral historical anecdote, after interviewing a medical man:

' In the town of Lancaster not above fifteen years ago, a quiet tradesman's family was sitting at tea one evening, when their parlour door was suddenly burst open, and a black human head rolled along the floor up to their feet! In an instant they had all burst away from the room, frenzied with fear and horror'

Half an hour later, they went back into the room. Amazingly, the place was completely normal, and there was no sign of a head. The tale was spread around and it made the regional newspapers, and so everyone was talking about the supernatural experience and lamenting the horrible experience the poor folk had had. There appeared to be no explanation, but the writer adds this:

'Is it therefore to be considered as inexplicable? By no means. The present Professor knows perfectly how it was that the frightful spectacle was presented. he was then a student of surgery, residing in the house of the tradesman in question. Having attended a poor negro servant on his deathbed in the town hospital, he had cut off the head of the deceased in order to make some investigation of the nature of the fatal *disease. Carrying the dismal object home in a handkerchief, he happened to make a slip in going down the slope which led to the door of his lodging.'*

Now, this demolishes the paranormal tale, but the interest here is in the fact that people (and the press) believed it to be possible – that is, for a head to arrive into a parlour and roll across the floor. So in a sense we have a ghostly tale that is not a ghostly tale, but it tells us a lot about just how far the human imagination will go to accept the most unlikely event.

HANGMAN'S HANDS

On September 20th, 1932, John Ellis came home to his house in Rochdale, with some strong drink in him. He decided to sit in a chair and there he dozed off. Later he woke up and his wife brought him some tea, and he then lit a pipe and sat in the front room quietly. His wife was sewing and his daughter was upstairs. All seemed peaceful, but that was soon to end.

Ellis went to the kitchen, grabbed a razor and went as though to attack his poor wife with it. He said, ' I'll cut your head off first!' The wife, Annie, dashed from the house and ran to her son's house to get help. The daughter, Ivy came down to see what was wrong and her father then held the razor to her face, saying, ' I can't cut your mother's head off, I'll cut yours off first.'

Eventually another son, Austin, came to the house and he was faced with the terrible sight of his father slitting his own throat and falling down. Austin ran for a doctor. But when the doctor arrived it was too late to help. John Ellis was dead. He had tried to kill himself before and failed. This time he had succeeded. This might have been just one more sad suicide with a few paragraphs devoted to the tale in the local paper. But John Ellis, barber in Rochdale, was also the nation's official hangman.

This was the man who had hanged such infamous people as Roger Casement, Dr Crippen, Frederick Seddon and Ethel Major. All this had taken its toll on his mental strength and as someone commented at the inquest, he hadn't really slept for months. Ellis had cracked, burnt out and with his nerves shattered. Many hangmen turned to alcohol and others took or tried to take their own lives. Ellis had carried on with his demanding and traumatic part-time job for years and finally his mind had snapped.

But is his spirit truly dead and gone? The Rochdale Observer reported in 2008 that at Susan Cotton's florist shop there is something there that is not a living being, and the place is where Ellis had his barber's shop. Susan's partner told the press: 'A few things happened... I felt a hand on my shoulder so I turned to see who it was, but then I realised I was the only person in the shop. It wasn't a weak hand. It was very firm and pushing.' He added that he had had his 'backside pinched' as well.

Susan and her partner had no idea of the place's history when they arrived, but every now and then people come to see the shop. Susan put the number back on the door so true crime enthusiasts who came could plainly see that

the address was 413 Oldham Road. Bravely, they want to know more about Ellis. It would come as no surprise if the couple experienced the ghost of a dog, because Ellis's old dog, Bob, pined and would not eat in the days before his master's body was interred. He sat outside the room where the coffin lay, sadly missing his friend.

A sketch of the Rochdale hangman, done by Laura Carter. His end was tragic, after the stresses and pressures of being the public executioner.

HOBSTONES AND BLACKO

By Lake Burwain off the Burnley-Skipton road is a farm reckoned by some to be one of the land's leading paranormal hot-spots. Once again, as so often in this context, we have the word hob, because this is Hobstones farm. The whole area is potentially eerie and deep in a dark history. The word 'Burwain' means a burial ground. The farm is very old, probably sixteenth century, and was once the home of the Royalist family, Parker in the Civil War. Colonel Parker was in a scrap with the Parliamentarians here and there have been sightings of Roundhead troops.

But the really intriguing story of Hobstones concerns something that happened in the 1950s: the inhabitant of the farm was at the toilet when he saw before him a tiny man in monk's clothes, and the figure had a badly severed arm; blood was pouring from it. Then the dwarf disappeared. Why there should be any connection with monks is a mystery. Yet that was not the end of the troubles, because twenty years later the tenants were the victims of a poltergeist. Accounts of this reign of terror included stones coming down stairs, knocks and smashed glass. What needs to be stressed here is that this is not just another random tale for tourists and hikers: matters were so bad that the Rector of Colne, the Rev. Noel Hawthorne, was called, to perform an exorcism. The exorcism appears to have been successful.

Not far away from the farm is Blacko Tower. One tradition says that this is the Malkin Tower of the Pendle witches, but that has not been substantiated.

Blacko, around six miles from Burnley, is a mystery, but one established fact is that it was built by Jonathan Stansfield, a grocer, ostensibly so he could see his girlfriend at Gisburn; this didn't work though because it was not high enough. It seems to be only half-finished.

It may be, as some writers have suggested, that Blacko, like Epworth in Lincolnshire, is on Ley Lines; these are energies aligned in the earth, detected by various means, including by dowsing (a largely little understood pursuit). It may well be a site with ancient origins related to such things as druid worship, but there does not seem to be a body of ghost lore linked to it. If this is the same as Malkin Tower, then it is traditionally alleged to be the place where Old Demdike gathered his witches' coven. There does seem to be, despite Harrison Aisnworth's legends, a record of such a meeting at that tower in 1612 of friends of the witches who had been lately arrested and who were languishing in gaol.

Whether there is a link between Ley Lines and hauntings is open to question; evidence with dowsing does seem to point to stones charged with electro-magnetism. As peter Underwood wrote on this:' John Mitchell... has discovered scores of paths of power that could be of value to the archaeologist, the psychical researcher and the occultist.' One thing is for sure: walkers on the route that takes in Blacko and Hobstones generally don't like to hang around for too long there. Blacko Tower stands like a malevolent entity, dominating the view, partly like a beacon and partly a dark marker of something we can never fully understand about that few square miles of ancient rock and its generations of farmers and labourers.

DE QUINCEY AND THE DOCTORS

In 1800, the famous writer Thomas de Quincey enrolled at Manchester Grammar School. He is famous as the author of the classic work on opium, Confessions of an English Opium Eater, but there is much more in that work than simply an account of what that drug does to the mind and body. There is a great deal in the book about paranormal experience, and De Quincey explains the Lancashire element in this: 'The southern section of that district, about eighteen or twenty miles long, which bears the name of Furness, figures in the eccentric geography of English law as a section of Lancashire, though separated from that county by Morecambe Bay; and therefore, as Lancashire happened to be my native county, I had from childhood on the strength of this mere legal fiction, cherished as a mystic privilege some fraction of denizenship in the little fairy domain...' He tends to be rather wordy, but his statement is basically that he had a psychic dimension to his character, tied in some way to his Lancashire roots. He had regular 'dream fugues' as he called them, such as this vision, following some meditations on sudden death:

'Sweet funeral bells from some incalculable distance, wailing over the dead that die before the dawn, awakened me as I slept in a boat moored to some familiar shore. The morning twilight even then was breaking; and by the dusky revelations when it spread,

I saw a girl, adorned with a garland of white roses… running along the solitary strand… Her running was the running of panic; and often she looked back as to some dreadful enemy in the rear. But when I leapt ashore, and followed in her steps to warn her of a peril in front, alas she fled from me as if from some other peril…'

De Quincey saw such things even before he took opium, and thanks to research by Simon Wilson writing in The Fortean Times, we have a fascination Manchester connection as part of a theory to explain what happened to Thomas de Quincey. Wilson points out that a Manchester doctor called John Ferriar wrote a book on apparitions, published in 1813, called An Essay towards a Theory of Apparitions. Wilson explains: ' Ghosts, he argues, are due to a "partial affection of the brain,Aù which leaves the witnesses sane but causes their senses to create illusory objects. Most influentially, he maintains that an inflammation of the brain may cause recollected images to be conjured up so that they are 'seen' again.'

The conclusion is that stomach problems may actually create the things we call apparitions. This suggests that ghosts are of a material, not spiritual origin. As Wilson says, it means that ghosts are produced 'when our bodies override our minds.' As far as De Quincey is concerned, his reasons for taking opium were to find ways of reducing or removing his 'visions.' The author described these visions or hallucinations as 'Visions as ugly as phantasms or ghosts, as ever haunted to couch of Orestes.' In fact, De Quincey does write about the results of taking opium on his digestive tract: he noted 'the ravages in the great central organ, the stomach.'

Dr Ferriar was a leading light in the Manchester Literary and Philosophical Society and Wilson notes that the author may even have seen and met the doctor. Ferriar, (1761-1815) is a major figure in the history of Manchester's medical and social history. After working in the fight to treat typhus, he moved on to an interest in mental illness, and he applied what would now be called psychiatric methods of therapy. As De Quincey, even as a teenager, moved in literary and intellectual circles, he may well have met Ferriar at the Manchester Coffee House on Mosley Street because that was the venue for the meetings of the private society of thinkers and medical men of the city, men who also founded the Portico Library. Ferriar was chairman in the years 1806 – 1815.

But what does Ferriar and all this theory mean for the 'apparitions' seen by De Quincey? Simon Wilson suggests that, '… his disordered senses, body and mind, were symptoms of a spiritual disorder, a crisis of the soul in which mere material nature claimed its right to generate not only his imagination but his very being.' In plain English, this is a line of thought about ghosts that explains them by saying that the living being experiencing the ghost really has something amiss with his or her balance of physical and spiritual health – that is, they may be depressed, they may be feeling low and vulnerable, and so on.

The only way to follow this up would be to research just how many people reporting apparitions had some kind of illness. I guess that would take years.

A BLACKBURN TALE

In 1887 a writer for the North Eastern Daily Gazette reported on a spate of sightings of a ghost in Blackburn, at Mount Pleasant. Several people were telling the press and the authorities about the mysterious figure seen in several different places, and the first point the reporter made was that 'This particular ghost does not take its walks abroad at the orthodox hours, ‚Äùo'er night's black arch the keystone,Äù - at any hour after nine o'clock at night. Nor has it any particular rendezvous...it is one of those obliging ghosts which is everywhere in turn and nowhere long..'

The tone of the report is tongue-in-cheek and satirical, but beneath that there was clearly a general panic in the town; the most sightings were in a graveyard:

'According to the statements of some of the residents, the ghost has been seen on several occasions stalking over the lonely tombs, and one man solemnly asserts that he was going home late one night and he was passing the gates of Holy Trinity church when he was suddenly rooted to the spot by something white gliding past him....'

The cynical writer tries to demolish all accounts but has to retell what was supposed to have happened nevertheless, as in this report: ' Three men were returning home last Saturday night when a whitish light was seen moving slowly at a distance... the Dutch courage of the trio began to ooze out as a very uncomfortable rate... they went helter-skelter down the road as fast as their legs could carry them.'

Other reports were about the appearance of a female shape, and it appeared inside a house. The man present at the time could no nothing but scramble under his table. When the man gathered his courage and came out, the ghost had gone. The writer of the report concludes that 'these are only some of the tales... the most absurd rumours are flying about and there is undoubtedly a certain amount of fear, if not terror, in the district.'

Of course, being a man of reason in the Victorian heyday of belief in empirical science, he could offer no explanation but boyish pranks by some locals. But more seriously, there were so many accounts given to police and parson that groups of people ventured out to do their own version of a paranormal investigation; the only problem was that, in an age when there was still plenty of superstition mixed with the fear, some men took cudgels and sticks with them, just to feel safer.

There appear to be no reports about how this strange affair ended.

Part III

EERIE DISTURBANCES IN THE WORKPLACE

THE STOCKHAM NAVVY

It is well established that the 'navvies' who worked on the railways in Victorian times were tough; it would have taken something extraordinarily frightening to move them. But on this occasion that is exactly what happened

In November, 1847 work on the railway near Stockham was stopped for a while, except for a few navvies who did some minor digging to some areas away from the others, close to a tunnel. Now, just a month before this, a man had been killed by a rockfall in that tunnel. The men set to work, and after a while, they felt sure that they heard the sound of a pickaxe coming from the place where the man had died. But there was a continuous high wind, so the sound could have been caused by that, in some way. They were so intrigued and troubled by this that they decided the best move was for one of them to go down to the place.

One man said that he 'feared nor man nor devil' and down he went. He had to be let down a shaft, and so a rope was tied to his waist. But before the man reached the bottom there was a frantic pulling on the rope and they heard demented cries from below. The newspaper report tells what happened: ' The man was pulled up instantly, with a countenance pale as death on which terror and consternation were strongly depicted. To the almost gasping enquiry of "What is it? What hast 'a seen?,Äù he related that, no sooner had he got to the bottom than he plainly saw the white, pale face of the dead man.'

The man had known the dead man, and so he was sure of the sight. News soon spread and there was talk of 'The railway ghost' for miles around. But then doubt was cast on the tale, and to this day we have no idea whether or not this was a trick, but another man was lowered and he came up with a new tin powder left in a rickety position. The report on that was that it could have resembled a man's face. But the jury is out. It surely would have taken something totally unnerving to make a hard man like that shriek in fear. It would surely take more than a simple object in the dark to scare a tough guy like a railway navvy.

AIRPORT GHOSTS

It has been well established that hauntings tend to be recorded regularly at the various former RAF bases across the country. Lincolnshire and North Yorkshire have a very large number of these, but in Lancashire we have the building at Manchester airport, described by Andrew Green in 1971 as being that of Claridge and Co. It was formerly the base of 613 Manchester Squadron of the RAF. But as Green noted, a number of staff at the time reported seeing what they described as 'an old man.'

Matters were so extreme that at the time the police were called on one occasion: objects were moved without any apparent volition and noises were heard from an empty room. It must have seemed like a very inept burglary, but of course the police found nothing.

Some of the most vivid accounts reported at the time Green wrote were of the old man being seen by an import clerk, who said that the figure was sitting in a store room, a shape that disappeared when access was made. Then on a night shift a number of workers saw the old man again, this time walking with bare feet across a room. Others backed up the same kind of apparition, including a report by a policeman.

As Green joked at the time, the thought of a ghostly cargo raised too many 'unanswered questions.'

PENNIES FROM HEAVEN

Falling coins, as noted in the earlier story from Mains Hall, are not so rare in unexplained events. But in 1981 there was an exceptional case of this 'manner from heaven' phenomenon. At the church of St Elizabeth at Reddish, Manchester, a large quantity of silver and copper coins fell in the churchyard.

The vicar, the Rev Graham Marshall, went to investigate and he came across two pounds in various coins. The most remarkable aspect of this was that many coins were not simply lying on the ground, but were embedded in the earth, by the edge. As The Fortean Times reported in 2010, there have been similar fallings reported in Gateshead and Ramsgate.

There have been several similar tales in recent times, including one experience from Columbus, Ohio, by a man who felt showers of coins falling by him as he walked around a mall. One explanation, described by several commentators, is that coins are one of many kinds of apports - items related to so -called supernatural hot spots. Rose Ellen Guiley has written that these are often rough-edged, as if they had been 'vigorously rubbed by a coarse sanding-block' and she described a fall of coins all from the 50s and 70s all falling to the ground in one of her cases. She adds that they may be an example of a 'trickster prank' common in poltergeist activity.

STEPHEN WADE

'JANE' AT THE RAILWAY INN

The railway from Waterfoot to Rawtenstall was opened in 1848 and near Newchurch station there was the Moulders Arms. It appears that this later became the Railway Inn and that has been a hot spot for a haunting

Forty years ago, at this pub in Waterfoot, the landlord reported to Andrew Green the presence of a ghost on his premises; it was not just any old spirit – it was familiarly known as 'Jane' by the landlord and others. Jane tended to walk through a bedroom and then into a wall. The disturbance does not end there, however, because the troublesome entity tended to take away the bed clothes as well. A Mr Cormack told Green that several guests had said that bed clothes had mysteriously disappeared in the night.

One guest said that he had seen Jane walk through the room and that she had definitely been close up to him. There has even been a voice calling to the owners. Everything about this would suggest the established pattern of a movement into a solid wall happening where there had once been open space. This would be a useful theory, because there was a bricked-up portion of the building at the time.

STEPHEN WADE

TOO MANY GHOSTS AT THE OLD MAN AND SCYTHE

This pub at Bolton is very old, with a cellar going back to 1251, so it compares in age to the famous trip to Jerusalem Inn at Nottingham. The main building was created in 1636. The place has the distinction of being included in Derek Acorah's collection of haunted places in Britain collected in Haunted Britain and Ireland. He comments that 'Even though the Old Man and Scythe has a bloody, troubled past... the staff are keen to point out that the pub is a happy, lively place to visit.' This needs to be said, because the track record is grim.

As so often in Lancashire, the roots of the alleged activity relate to the Civil War. At the Bolton massacre in 1644 hundreds were killed- and then there was an execution outside the place when the Earl of Derby was beheaded. One of the most prominent hauntings is that of a case related to a chair which is the one he is supposed to have sat in before death.

The Most Haunted crew have visited, and found that an investigation could not go ahead because the place was not suitable for recording, as there are no doors on the haunted rooms. It has to be said that the old Earl is maybe happy at not being disturbed. One of the most horrible tales related about the pub is that of a woman who left her seat and saw that there was blood on her hands; it appeared that this had dripped from above. It certainly is an epicentre of activity – over twenty sightings have been reported there.

SUNLIGHT HOUSE STORIES

Steve Mera conducted an investigation into Sunlight House in Deansgate, Manchester, and he reported his findings in Ghost Voices magazine in 2009. The building was built in 1932 by Joseph Sunlight, made of steel and concrete and then with an exterior of Portland stone; It has an art deco design, and was meant to be the first skyscraper in the North, reaching up 40 storeys, but that never happened. It was renovated in 1997, and has houses, shops and offices

The site of Sunlight House was formerly some lodging houses and a rag dealer worked there too. Steve has looked into the history of the house and discovered a Mr Zchovsky, a Russian businessman who once owned it. He died in 1978 and his grave is unknown

Within the frame of the building's interior there are old lifts and some Gothic architecture. But in human terms, the various inhabitants have recorded troubled histories, such as a suicide attempt in 1964 and a suicide in which a man hanged himself on the thirteenth floor

What prompted Steve and his team to go there was of course the usual impetus – a range of testimonies by people who had worked there. These included a man who saw all the light go out and then heard a 'rasping male voice about three feet behind him.' There was also statement from a woman recalling that she had been washing her hands when she sensed another hand by her side, and when she turned she saw an old man looking at her.

The most vivid account came from a former security guard, who said, 'Our ghost followed me down the stairs from floor 4 ‚Äî1 at about 03.15 hours. This time he was not solid, just a shape and a hair-pricking sensation. I stopped on level 2 to try to talk to him. Again, he vanished...'

The team took video cameras and other equipment, and the usual glitches occurred, including incorrect functions of the cameras, and audio equipment being turned off. But Steve concluded that there were several positive results, confirming the place as a hot-spot for hauntings. He wrote: 'We had obtained strange balls of light on video camera film something odd caught on camera...The phenomena noted from these incidents during the vigil and past reports all seem to suggest that the building is very much haunted...'

GIANT IN THE HEADLIGHTS

This is a tale told by writer, Richard Whittington-Egan, expert and chronicler of Liverpool and the Mersey. He wrote that he and a friend, Routledge, were to 'keep a date with a ghost' one night. The search began as they sat in the car with the lights of Speke Airport in the distance, looking out over s stretch of waste land. They could see the river in the dark, and the skeleton of a ship that was beached.

Richard was there because his friend had recalled a night in 1951 when he was breaking up an old German barque and he and his sister and wife had got into their car. It had been a dark night and all three stepped out of the car to look at the ship, with the headlights on full beam. Then, Mrs Routledge saw a dark shape across the stretch of land. They all looked to see a huge figure of a man coming towards them from the waste land. Routledge said that the man was huge: 'He looked at least six foot six and I was particularly struck by his hair which stood up from his head in a great bush four or five inches high.'

Richard explained that they saw the figure pass right through the headlights of the car without breaking their beam, and then he disappeared before he reached a corrugated - Iron fence.

Richard and Routledge, then, were out to see if the figure would appear

124

again. Nothing really happened, although Richard did say that he detected a movement, and Routledge said that the location was exactly where the giant had risen from. All Richard could say was ' I came away with the impression that we had been on the brink of some strange experience.'

GEORGE AT THE ADELPHI

Afigure known as George has been seen at the most famous hotel in Liverpool, and we might speculate as to who this might be, given that suicides notoriously haunt the places of the final moments, then some history might explain 'George.'

It is not widely known that the end of the story of one of the most intriguing and celebrated murder cases of the Twentieth Century happened in Liverpool at the grand and stylish Adelphi Hotel in 1942. It was there that Sir Jock delves Broughton took his own life. The story was that of the murder of Lord Erroll in Kenya in 1941, whose body was found in a car in January of that year, with a bullet lodged in his brain.

The irony of the place of his death is not hard to miss. The Adelphi is huge and palatial; a visit there now evokes the glamour and excitement of the great age of the ocean liners; in the 1940s it would have had some of that glamour. In the midst of the ballroom dances and the ebb and flow of immigrants and fugitives from war, the inscrutable old drinker and bon viveur exited the world. There is something fitting there in the effete and somehow pathetic figure dying in that place

In the film White Mischief, the murder and the tale of the affair that caused it is told with high drama and passion; there were certainly elements of that in the real tragedy of this threesome of older man, attractive young wife and dashing lover. But there was also a large element of what we now see as sordid and sad. The affair is all the more fascinating because Broughton was the only real suspect and yet the murder is unsolved to this day. Broughton insisted on his innocence, writing to an aunt in 1941 he wrote, 'I was just a victim of unfortunate circumstances... some clever person took advantage of an unrivalled opportunity of getting rid of Erroll and... throwing all suspicion on me.'

'Jock' as he was known, had married Diana Caldwell in Durban in November 1940 at a registry office. From there they went to Kenya. He had promised to let her have five thousand pounds a year. Then she went on to enjoy herself with Lord Erroll, and Jock's torment began. There was something inevitable about the course of Erroll's life, from the affair through to his being shot on the Ngong to Nairobi road. What made Broughton so intriguing a character was the fact that he had been hired by MI6, and that he had a Somali driver who worked for him, leading to the theory that this driver could easily have been in the back of the car that night, and could have done the required execution.

Broughton's descent after the acquittal from the murder charge led him to Liverpool. He had always been a heavy drinker, but now he was intensely so, and he boarded ship for Liverpool in October, 1942 in a rotten state; he was still full of venom, and cabled his friend Colville from the ship saying of his former wife, Diana, 'You've got the bitch, now buy her the kennel.' He was angry and vengeful, writing that he would let it be known that Diana had perpetrated an insurance false claim some years before. The desperate and raging Lord must have felt that this was his final journey: he had only been in Liverpool for just over a month when he took his own life. A morphine overdose was to end the life of this notorious aristocrat.

Even in death, however, there was mystery around the man. The Liverpool coroner had been given possession of a letter written by Broughton to be given to him after the man's death, and the coroner never made the contents of this public. But with regard to the anticlimax of the manner of Broughton's death in Liverpool, it must be said that according to one line of thought, the whole thing was in fact a murder and had been fabricated as a suicide. The theory goes that Broughton knew too much from his past in espionage and in terms of the politics of the time and place of his life in Africa. The outcome, if we believe this speculation, is that he had to be removed from the scene, and that the OSS (Office of Strategic Services) had made sure that a particular drug was taken that fateful night. As Errol Trzebinski has said, the Liverpool coroner would have been expected to know where the fatal drugs came from. Perhaps he had no idea. What we are left with is a spy story, one involving a man who was maybe involved in a 'hit' job of Errol, but who was just a pawn. Here was a man who was suspected of being a fraud, and surely weighed down by guilt.

His character has been summed up by historian David Cannadine in this way: '... another dim and vain Etonian, with fifteen thousand acres in Cheshire and Staffordshire... He evaded military service in 1914 on the grounds of sunstroke, and brought the Spring Valley estate in Kenya in 1923.

The Adelphi hotel, Liverpool, once a popular place for those about to board the liners.

His purpose in life was to have a good time.'

There was no good time that night in the Adelphi when he reached the end of the line. If it was suicide, it was a crime of course, at that time. Until 1961 that kind of death was an offence in the eyes of the law. The grand, palatial Adelphi, pride of the city in several incarnations since James Radley built the first one in 1826, including the version that was fairly new when Jock arrived – the delight of the great hotelier, Arthur Towle – and he would have been shuddering with shame at the stigma of a suicide in those marble walls.

Is 'George' the shade of the famous suicide?

BRANNIGANS

Anyone who watched the Most Haunted programmes on Living TV will recall vividly the investigation at Brannigan's club in Manchester. The main reason for this is the phase of the vigil in which Derek Acorah and others climb to the highest attic room in the neighbouring disused chapel and Derek claims he can smell the essence of vomit when a baby is sick. Then others smell it too.

When they finally stood in the attic room, it is revealed to Derek that there was a notoriously hard, cruel character associated with the place, a certain Godfrey, who was reputedly held in spirit there by clergymen; the tradition is that the man killed children; two of the children were allegedly called Peter and Elizabeth, and amazingly, the Most Haunted team had the sound of a child crying on their EVP recording.

In a discussion forum on this, several respondents considered the voice on the tape to be that of an older child, and several people wanted a clearer, cleaned-up version of the recording to be available. This all raises the question of voice phenomena generally; one of the earliest assertions of paranormal voice recordings was as far back as 1959 when a Swedish film producer said that he had voices of dead people recorded. Theories then came forward, mainly that the subconscious mind of a living person can send out messages. But as Peter Underwood has said, ' It is perhaps significant that the voices are often in more than one language, that they appear to be snatches of conversation rather than message...' That applies to the Brannigan material, as it is one statement in focus, perhaps repeated.

There has also been a poltergeist reported there, and at one time staff reported being pushed down stairs by the force; then there is, according to Derek Acorah, the ghost of a preacher from the Edwardian period called Samuel Collier.

As a coda to the Most Haunted time there, after the bar was closed, the group held a séance, and there was the sound of tiny feet heard walking around them, together with cold spots and a chilly wind.

SYKE LUMB FARM AND DILWORTH

In folklore, demons, sprites and goblins occur frequently, and in times gone by the rural communities had numerous tales of such evil spirits up to their frightening tricks. In Lancashire, even as recently as late Victorian times, there was a belief in goblins in some areas. In 1850, for instance, Syke Lumb Farm near Blackburn was well known to people in the area as a place when goblins were active.

A writer around that time reported:

'When in a good humour, this noted goblin will milk the cows, pull the hay, fodder the cattle, harness the horses, load the carts and stack the crops. When irritated by the utterance of some unguarded expression or remark of disrespect... the cream mugs are then smashed to atoms, no butter can be obtained, the horses and cattle are turned loose... and all the while the wicked imp sits grinning with delight on one of the crossbeams in the barn...'

Goblins, according to Brewer's Dictionary of Phrase and Fable, are: ' Familiar demons, according to popular belief, dwelling in private houses and chinks of trees, and in many parts miners attribute those strange noises heard in mines to them.'

Demons take all kinds of forms, we are told, including, at Samlesbury church near Preston, that of a 'demon pig' and also as the infamous 'Gabriel hounds' in the Cragg Vale area near Todmorden. There was also a legend there about a creature called a 'Lubbar Fiend' who could be found stretched out across the farm-house hearth.

Usually, tales of sprites, goblins and fairies relate to moral tales as well, as in this story sent to the journal Notes and Queries in 1853: 'Two men went poaching, and having placed nets or sacks over what they supposed to be rabbit-holes, but which were in reality fairy-holes, the fairies rushed into the sacks and the poachers, content with their prey, went home again. A fairy missing another in the sack, called out, "Dick, where art thou?,Äù to which the other replied, ‚ÄùIn a sack/ on a back Riding up Barley Brow,Äù - and the poachers ran home in fear.

Goblins are a variant of the word 'Hob' and in Lancashire and Yorkshire we find place names with the 'hob' affix included, as in Hob Bridge at Gatley. Similar is the word 'boggart' as in Boggart Hill Clough, and the origin of that relates to the word 'bug' - ultimately coming from the Celtic word 'bwg' for ghost in general.

What are we to make of these legends? In earlier writing, they appear to have had a genuine influence on attitudes and behaviour, and who is to deny that in the mists of unrecorded time there were not manifestations which are at the root of these beliefs?

A related notion is of the boggart, and one of the best-known Lancashire stories on this theme comes from Dilworth on Longridge Fell. On a bank near Rafe Radcliffe's Farm there is a large stone with these words written on it:

Rauffe Radcliffe laid this

Stone to lye for ever A.D. 1655

Tradition has it that this huge stone was placed there to hold still a boggart, but in one of the classic works on Lancashire folklore, *Lancashire Legends* by Harland and Wilkinson, we have:

'Tradition decrees this spot to have been the scene of a cruel and barbarous murder, and it is stated that this stone was put down in order to appease the restless spirit of the deceased, which played its nightly gambols long after the body had been 'hearsed in earth'. A story is told of one of the former occupants of Written Stone Farm [an alternative name] who, thinking That the stone would make a capital buttery stone, removed it into the house ... the result was that the indignant or liberated spirit would never suffer his family to rest...'

Later writers have stressed that the stone would have been impossible to shift, and yet the tradition has it that the unfortunate man replaced the stone somehow.

BLACKPOOL TOWER

There is no doubt that Blackpool is brimming with stories of hauntings. Why this should be is not entirely explicable, but a number of writers on the paranormal have listed and described countless examples of apparitions and poltergeists around the town. In my experience there are a few such places, somehow attracting the apports of spirits and also apparently holding past energies – in abundance. Epworth in Lincolnshire is such a place, and also York. Blackpool is in that category, without a doubt.

In this body of lore and oral history stands the Tower, opened in 1894, naturally inspired by the famous Eiffel Tower in Paris, and reaching to a height of 518 feet. This was the brainchild of John Bickerstaff, a mayor of the town, who initiated the project with an investment from his own purse, starting with the formation of the Blackpool Tower Company in 1891. The architects were Maxwell and Tuke, and the cost was almost £300,000 – a massive structure of over five thousand square metres. Was there maybe a dark foreboding about its future when it in fact in caught fire in 1897? Whatever the truth of that, there was no problem when the new tower complex was declared open in 1992, with Princess Diana officiating.

In the celebrated ballroom, forever associated with the organist, Reginald Dixon, there was another fire, in 1956; but it never stopped progress. The whole complex, including the ballroom and circus, have entered popular imagination and the word iconic has now to be applied. Yet beneath all this public history, there is another – a chronicle of strange events and of course, hauntings. Of the many instances, there is the appearance of Bickerstaff, the presiding genius loci of the place. Many staff have given accounts of seeing his spirit walk the place – a man in Victorian clothes. But most interesting is surely the account of a woman given by Darren Ritson. He recounts that the woman in question was on her way to the girls' room when she saw a shape along the corridor. When it came closer she said that is was 'something like a human shape' and that it wore a top hat. She had actually walked towards the shape, at first assuming it was a living human being, just another member of staff.

Another report is from the South King Street area, where, in a place which was once a tobacco warehouse, workers in a cellar felt they were not alone. An old cutting revealed that there was supposedly a restless spirit there, and there was even a name – Laura Schoons – a person from Scarborough. Darren Ritson adds that still today staff feel there is a presence and that they are being watched.

Of all Blackpool ghosts, surely the poltergeist at the Illuminations department on Rigby Road is the most shocking and persistent. Cold spots and voices heard have continued, and a medium who was brought in made contact and produced a name for the entity – being called Ted. This activity has lasted for some time and continues to annoy and disturb.

Finally, with Blackpool in focus, Darren Ritson's own experience in the Ghost Train is truly remarkable and well documented. He was in search of a ghost known as 'Cloggy' because staff have reported that they have heard footsteps and even been touched by this entity. Darren took a team with him, and they split into two, setting off not long before eleven at night, walking into the tunnel. The first remarkable happening was a loud beating sound like a motor warming up, but later he was told that no mechanisms were in action at the time. Then, later, there were knocks, bumps and lights evident inside.

After that, a séance was held in situ, and Darren reported that after addressing himself to Cloggy, asking for a sign, a door shook and rattled. He asked again, provoking a response and he got one – something touched him on the shoulder. He really pushed it far into the area of a demand when he asked for the well known footsteps, but he got them alright: he heard the sound of footsteps echoing along the dark passage.

Blackpool is also a very special place for medium, Ian Lawman, who explained his link to the place and in particular to Blackpool legend, Charlie Cairoli: 'My awareness of my spiritual life goes back to when I was four. We all seem to be around that age in our first recall of memory. In my case it began with visions of seeing people walk through walls, and I saw shapes and figures that were not really there. I was in a box room, and my room was above a staircase. I heard banging going on in my wardrobe. I was petrified. I used to run across to my sister's room for comfort. There was this clown with a pure-white powdered face, with red lipstick; his eyes were heavily blacked with mascara, and to me he had on what I can only call a dunce's hat.

That was my first experience of Charlie Cairoli's father. This brings me to the point where I have to explain about my spirit guide, Charlie. The figure in the wardrobe was his father, but today Charlie is with me. The Greeks used to think that we all have a spirit, a daemon (not to be confused with a demon). But whatever we want to call these spirits, the fact is that they are there for a reason. At four years old I had no understanding of this, of course, but today I know that Charlie took over from his father to be my special guide. Charlie died in 1980, and many people will know him most for his forty years of work at the Blackpool Tower Circus and from television. His rounded, smiley face and wonderful playful absurdity defined what we think of when we use the phrase 'circus clown.'

One day I plucked up the courage to open the wardrobe when I heard this noise, and there was this clown, juggling, and the balls were hitting the wood, so that was the source of the tapping noise. Was it a dream? No, when I was older I knew this was real. This figure was with me until I was around eleven. The wardrobe was alike a portal. The Charlie's father appeared. His father never spoke. He just played games and entertained. Charlie soon told me who he was. I believe that we are all born with spirit guides and they come and go, but guardian angels stay with us. Charlie's father, I believe, was there to help me have a childhood, to laugh and giggle, because a lot of that was not there in me. Everything was focused on my sister. Charlie then came in because he felt I was ready to communicate to him and to the spirit world. He never had a white face. He was and is, a real person. He never spooked me like his father.

Charlie said he came from France, and that he was here to help me and to be behind me to somehow share in making my life meaningful. I believe that he is here to continue the childish humour in me, and to sustain that ability to guide other people's lives.

Obviously I've found out more about him since. I know that he had a children's show on television called Right Charlie! and that he was known as 'The King of Clowns' but all that is only a sidelight. To me he is special, and his presence is an invaluable part of everything I do in my spiritual being.

BOOTH HALL TALES

The Booth Hall infirmary for children was, in 1929, the third largest children's hospital in the land. A description written at that time noted: ' The infirmary is unique in respect of its 204 open-air beds in separate cubicles into which all newly-admitted patients are placed for a period of quarantine.' It included a convalescent home, and there was provision then for home visits after return home. At that time the boast was that it was the first place in the north of England to provide sunlight treatment for orthopaedic cases, enough to treat 300 children each week. It had been in existence since 1908 when it was made to be part of the Prestwich Union. It still functions today, and like most such institutions, it has its paranormal tales.

Reports of unexplained events include sightings of a shadowy figure, and also toilets flushing by themselves and noises coming from tenantless rooms. The most common experience is the sight of what appears to be a figure of a janitor who worked there in past times. One respondent who worked there some time ago verified that she had seen an apparition of a small boy wearing the type of 'long short trousers like they used to have, and pressed, just like they were when I was young. The description was of 'a boy playing or tugging at his mouth, as if he had a great pain there...'

A similar note in response to an appeal for stories brought a memory of 'something following me in a corridor, and like a murmur, as if someone was asking for help.' The various memoirs do have things in common, as if the visions were repeated, and that makes for more credence of course.

Patients can be treated by a Physician or Surgeon of their own choice whom they are responsible for the charges made, which are on a scale as proportionately below those received for private nursing home practice as are the auxiliary hospital charges themselves. The scheme has met with considerable success, especially for surgical and maternity cases.

An atmospheric image of a troubled location. 1930's picture from a brochure.

OCTAGON THEATRE

The Octagon Theatre in Bolton, established in 1967, includes the Bill Naughton Theatre, in honour of the successful author and playwright. The ghost there is apparently that of a wardrobe mistress. She has been seen walking around, and also at a sewing machine; her name was Vida, and she died whilst at work. Strangely, Derek Acorah, though he mentions this in his own reference work of northern hauntings, has no personal memory of anything seen or heard in the theatre.

But several tales seem to agree that the woman – also called Fida by some – is almost certainly the figure seen on several occasions. One sighting even places her in the ticket office, so it seems that she was someone who liked to be in control and enjoyed some variety in her working life as well

THE OLD ORIGINAL

This is a very old pub in Oldham, and records agree that the ghost there is of someone called Eliza Jane Mackay, who was a customer back in Victorian times. In line with so many hauntings, this is a murder story, because Eliza was killed and then thrown into a nearby well. The most common manifestation is of a woman screaming, and reporters surmise that this could be the sound of Eliza's screams as she was killed. However, another tradition has the girl take her own life by throwing herself in the well.

She is apparently seen as a shadowy figure, always seen in the same part of the interior, although it is claimed that she has been seen in the cellar too. In fact, the story will live on as long as the report of the death, from the local newspaper, remains on the wall for all to read. Eliza was seen regularly by Mrs Vera Marner, who was the landlady there in the 1970s.

BILL O' JACKS

Arguably, this is the most sensational and dramatic unsolved northern murders ever perpetrated, and the spirits of the murdered men are reputedly out on the moors. Known also as the Moorcock Inn case or the Marsden Moor or Greenhill murders, this is the tragic tale of a double murder at the Lonely Inn on Saddleworth moor in 1832 in which several facts and clues seem to have a definite bearing on the resolution, but eventually come to nothing.

The victims were eighty-four-year-old William Bradbury, landlord of the inn (known as Bill o'Jacks) and his son Thomas, aged forty-six. They had been shot and there had been a massive struggle, as Thomas was a giant of a man who was in the habit of throwing nuisance drinkers over the back wall. This strongly built, powerful man was shot along with his father and Bill , before he died, made the intriguing statement that 'Pat' or 'Pad' did the deed. Now, the complication comes in the detail that there were Irish workers nearby ('paddies') and also that there were local pedlars near called Burn Platters. A man called Reuben Platt had listened to the old man foolishly talk about his stash of money in the bar, and he was suspected. But there was a major suspect in the person of Red Bradbury, of a local criminal family. His brother Tom had been prosecuted for poaching by the Bradbury family who owned the pub (no relation) and was due to appear in court in Pontefract the day after the murder.

The murder scene was horrendous. Poor Mary, the old man's granddaughter, walked in on a scene of carnage. The big man had obviously fought for his life, and the room was wrecked.

Until the time that the Moorcock was pulled down in 1937, the murder and the surrounding area had been the subject of morbid tourism and local folklore, with ghost stories attached to the tale as well. The best guide to this impact is perhaps the text on the tombstone of the victims in Saddleworth churchyard:

'Those who now talk of far-famed Greenfield's hills,

will think of Bill o'Jacks and Tom' Bills,

such interest did their tragic end excite,

that 'ere they were removed from human sight,

thousands on thousands daily came to see

the bloody scene of the catastrophe.'

Many walkers have claimed to see and feel a number of ghostly figures in that area, and certainly it was a place where one of the most brutal and violent killings in Britain took place. But Saddleworth generally has a very cluttered chronicles of all kinds of sightings. One of the most famous people to have a paranormal experience out there is Morrissey who, in 1989, reported seeing the ghost of a boy, wearing nothing but an anorak. He said that he and his friends saw this terrified figure run from the moors and come to their car, begging for help. This was on the Wessenden road, and

A cover of a local publication showing the widswept, lonely place.

he said that when they reached a phone box they rang to tell the police. When he returned there the next day, he found the spot deserted, without any pathways from which the boy could have come.

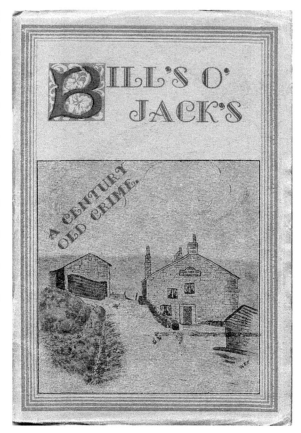

BOAR'S DEN

A writer of the 1850s gave his readers an extensive account of the Douglas Valley, stretching from Wigan to Hesketh Bank. He itemised a number of haunting traditions and luckily he captured some stories before they sank into oblivion, talking to older inhabitants in most cases.

His discovery of Boar's Den revealed a particularly disturbing tale. Boar's Den, as he wrote, is 'About three miles went of the Roman road which passes through Wigan and Standish, the elevation is about 320 feet above sea level. From this plateau a magnificent view presents itself at every point of the compass...' Close to the Den over the years, there have been a large number of bones, both of men and of animals, dug up; it has always been said that the spot was a sacred one for the Vikings, dedicated to the goddess Freya. In other words, it is the location of a tumulus.

An old man talking in the Victorian years recalled that when he was young he dug there and found what he called 'implements of war.' Whatever the origins of the haunting, it was not pleasant. The old man told the writer that at a gate by what was called Dangerous Corner he and his brother had seen 'a boggart.' He described this creature as 'going clanking and groaning round the field, in chains.' There was a house nearby called Boggart House, and one account has this:

'Some two years ago, the sickness of one of the inmates of Boggart House, the Visitations of the house ghost became so frequent and terrifying that the inhabitants finally fled in terror, and the house was empty at the time of my visit...'

Another old labourer there told the same investigator in 1860 that spirits were often seen at Hill House Farm, another place close to Boggart House.

The whole area is a hot spot of unexplained and disturbing activity, and Dangerous Corner was for many years a place people avoided; this story serves to back up the general atmosphere of Gothic horror the area nurtures and perhaps explains the dark foreboding mystery of the Corner:

'There is a story connected with dangerous Corner. A farmer in the neighbourhood whose wife had died, was "tekkin her to t'buryin',Äù when the carriers accidentally knocked the coffin against the wall in rounding Dangerous Corner. The corpse came to life again with the sudden shock and the wife returned alive to her home. Some time after she sickened and died; and as the funeral procession approached Dangerous Corner the husband said, "Now then lads, be careful you don't knock her agen t' corner this time...'

The investigator was told several tales of cries being heard at the Corner for years after.

SKULL HOUSE

Five minutes away from Appley Bridge station in the nineteenth century was Skull House, and even in 1860 it was hidden from view by new brick villas, but at the time there were still plenty of old farm houses there, and Skull House, when a writer visited there in that year, had just been repaired and stuccoed. The writer wrote an account of his visit:

'There used to be several aumbreys (recesses or pantries) in the kitchen wall and in one of these I have been shown a human skull which was kept in a box with a glass front. It was said that any attempt to remove this skull was always futile as it invariably returned. The skull is supposed to be that of a lady who was murdered in the house. On a recent visit to Skull House I find that the skull is no longer on view, the notoriety of the relic having been a nuisance to the inmates..'

The fact is that he was told by the people there that they were too 'afeared' to keep the skull because after being taken into light, 'someone or something paid us a visit that very same night Sir, and it was not pleasant to behold...'

MILEY TUNNEL GHOST

It is well established that railway lines have restless dead among their shady inhabitants. Deserted stations, disused lines, places where sad suicides have occurred – these all provide a wealth of railway tales, as in a recent report of a man doing some filming at Halsall Nature Reserve. He stood on an old railway bridge and as he filmed he heard the sounds of moving railway carriages beneath him. That would be a typical example. But Miley Tunnel is a very different matter.

This is part of what was a branch line, the route originally designed to transport stone from quarries ; but then the Preston and Longridge Railway was created in 1836. It was eventually closed in 1967. Part of the line was Miley Tunnel, and the ghost seen there is of a grey lady – a colour often seen from all kinds of time references of course. On this occasion, the woman was apparently pulled onto the rail track by a man at Deepdale station and she went under the wheels of the locomotive.

The man was arrested, as it appeared to be a homicide case, but no proof was produced that would have made him a killer; no evidence of an intention to kill was established. But there appears to be some kind of hex on the place: there have been other, more recent accidents, including that of a young man who fell onto the disused line not far away.

QUARRYMAN'S ARMS CELLAR

In October, 2009, Chris Hoper reported for The Lancahsire Telegraph on the strange happenings at The Quarryman's Arms in Blackburn. Staff had reported such odd events as gas being turned on and off, footsteps, and lights being interfered with. The publicans had only been there a short time, but things were so mad that they brought in a psychic medium to try to established what they had there.

The medium, Angela Riding, reported that she had made contact with a former worker there, and sure enough, there had been a violent death. She was sure that the restless spirit had fallen to its death down some steps. It is a very old pub, going back to the Eighteenth Century, so there is plenty of atmosphere down in the cellar, and orbs have been caught on film. A gas engineer who tried to work down there told the press that it was 'not threatening, just bizarre.'

The cellar ghost has been given a name: Albert Matt Regan, an employee there, asked Angela to come and try to give an explanation to what was happening. He told Chris Hopper that 'It is just as if Albert is larking about with us.'

This tale raises the subject of orbs, and there have been plenty of different explanations of what they might be. The rational mind simply says that they are particles of dust, but there is much more to them than that. Conventionally, many suggest that orbs are the first stage of a ghost manifestation. Alternatively, they may well be another variety of the shape we normally call a 'ghost' for the sake of immediate explanation. Interestingly in one Most haunted programme, a shape was caught on film which appeared to be an orb, but had within it a clearly defined human outline. Still the theories go on, but the fact is that, as with Albert, there are almost daily images of orbs on film across the world now, and not simply those produced by investigators.

THE MENTAL ASYLUM

I earlier mentioned the new hobby of urbexing, and this story comes in a way as something prompted by an urbexing exploration. It happened at the Whittingham mental Hospital. It is from a memory of working there, given by a Mr Butterfield.

What could be more spine-shivering than the thought of a rotting, abandoned mental hospital. It prompts all kinds of memories and images, from stories, film and popular narratives. According to one writer, abuses perpetrated there came out in the 1960s Whittingham Enquiry, so that adds to the expectancy

The place was opened officially in 1873, near Preston. It became known locally as the Duck Pond and was on a large scale: it was designed by Henry Littler of Manchester and eventually cost £338,000. It closed in 1995. At its most active and successful peak, the hospital had around 3,500 patients within its walls and was one of the largest institutions in Europe.

Mr Butterfield worked night shifts as a staff nurse, and his hours were from 7.30 p.m. to 7.30 a.m. and he told the Blogpreston site that ''If anything spooky was going to happen, it would happen during those hours.' He recalled two experiences for the site.

First there was the time he was sitting with a workmate about three in the morning. He said, 'We were chatting and my colleague suddenly went very quiet and I saw the look on her face change, just for a few seconds, and

I asked her what was wrong and she said she had seen a shape on my shoulder. She said it was like a monkey shape, and only there for a second...'

Mr Butterfield didn't feel anything, but the statement rocked him somewhat. But he was certainly shaken by his second experience. That concerned a long dark corridor which provided a short cut. He recalled that one night he boldly decided to go along that corridor and he felt that someone was watching him: 'The way the corridor was set up meant it had windows on either side that looked into old wards, and there were these wrought iron beds in there – old ones – and other stuff. Needless to say I walked very quickly...'

The ruin is within sight of the infamous Chingle Hall, so who knows where that line of thought might lead us...

RED ROCK

When medium Michelle Lee led an investigation into strange occurrences at the red Rock Inn at Padiham, she must have had no inkling of what was to emerge from the time there. She responded to the usual tales of noises, people being touched and so on, and her group, In Search of Spirit, were determined to test out the location with all the scientific back-up they had.

Michelle's report, published on the Lancashire website, begins with an immediate response to something: a 'female presence' and the description given is that she wore a molly cap and her hair was tucked up. The spirit was Mary, and she had been there in the 1860s. Michelle noted, ' She was quite strong in her energies... I felt a sudden surge of energy run through me.'

The group went upstairs and there the temperature dropped sharply. Then the presence of an older woman than Mary was sensed, and one member saw her, but it was the former who communicated and Michelle wrote that Mary had worked at a nearby mill and lived in the building that was today the inn. The spirit gave the name of Thomas Harwood, so there was a potential first step there for further research.

Later the group held a séance and an orb was caught on film, and the interesting aspect of that was that one group member said he felt that a male spirit was sitting near the door, and that was where the orb was pictured. In fact, it is worth noting that, as so many ghost sightings are in pubs and inns, a trend emerges, one in which there is a relation between society or conviviality and the cold presence of a soul in process of passing over or which is grounded within perceptible time-reference. It is as if the ghost wants to be part of the most 'alive' area, the most happily social element in the life it, he or she observes and sometimes participates in.

HAUNTED LIFT

The grand Birkdale palace hotel in Southport has known days of leisure and elegance; it was opened in 1866 and survived until the 1960s, having been used also as a rehabilitation centre for American airmen during the second world war. It was a very impressive place, on a twenty-acre site, with a reception room and 75 bedrooms

It has always had a very prominent ghost story attached to it: that of the supposed suicide of the architect, William Mangnall. It appears that recent research has shown that the man had a less dramatic and quite legal end: he died of consumption in Lord Street, Southport, in 1868.

Nevertheless, the hotel oft has been the focus of paranormal tales over the years; it is fair to say that the local oral history of the lift was boosted by the media, because the Southport Visitor featured the story back in 1969. The aura of menace over the left came from a report by workers there at the time who said that the lift was 'doing strange things.' The leader of the team organising the demolition, Jos Smith, said, ' Things began to happen soon after we started the job. First we were woken up by eerie voices and other strange noises in the middle of the night, and then the lift began to work by itself.'

This has been a feature of several reports and investigations: machinery working of its own accord. I have researched a report in Yorkshire, for instance, in which a juke box played after the power was switched off; there were four listeners who corroborated the story at the time.

A similar feature was noted at this hotel: the power for the lift had been cut off and it was even verified that the brakes were turned on; but this massive lift, weighing four tons, as the men reported at the time, went on 'merrily making its way between floors.' Jos added that all this was making his workers 'jittery.' The only way to stop it seemed to be to cut it free: it was removed from its holdings and that should have sorted the problem but it still moved! It shuddered down two floors.

The lift was not the only centre of activity. There were also experiences with sounds: voice and arguments were heard, and the sound of a stiletto heel was heard – a very distinctive, sharp and piercing noise of course. The Rochdale team played it safe and locked themselves in their rooms.

The myth of the suicide was at the time very powerful of course. Mr Mangnell was said to have been responsible for a major error – building the place so that it faced the wrong way. The urban myth was that the man had come to see his handiwork and noticed that the little, ordinary rooms looked out over the sea, while the top-class rooms were at the back. But later investigation cancelled this tale.

It has been pointed out that there is one small part of the hotel's total foundation still in existence: the Fishermen's Rest pub on Weld Road. Staff have reported the presence of a small girl there, and one worker told the press: 'You know there's something there, something watching you. The hairs stand up on the back of your neck.'

What could be the origin of any apparitions there? Researchers automatically look for trauma in the historical records, and sure enough, there was a coroner's inquest held at the pub in 1886 when a ship was wrecked off the coast and fourteen lifeboat men died. The pub's name is in honour of those brave men of the Southport and St Anne's Lifeboat.

ANTIQUES SHOP GHOST

Of all the locations were one might expect to see or sense the unexplained, surely antiques shops must be high on the list. After all, these are places were objects and possessions from years ago, linked for ever to human touch and use, are stored in a small space. If there is any substance in the 'preserved energy of grounded ghosts' thought then we would expect support and evidence from the antiques places.

Certainly one shop, in Morecambe, could be quoted in the evidence. The Southport Visitor reported on this in 2009, referring to the Morecambe Antiques Centre where a paranormal investigation team had been at work, and then the same was done at GB Antiques in Lancaster, with every hope of finding something interesting, because the owners had reported knockings and 'felt a presence' there.

The owner said that on one occasion he put a china clown ornament down on a table and then saw, to his horror, that it whizzed through the air and shattered. The ghosthunters from the Phoenix Group who went focused on an old seaman's chest as the epicentre of activity had much to say. They said, ' It is very rare to find energies or spirits connected with individual pieces of furniture... this is the first time we have found this..' Michelle Stavert of the group also commented that she thought the chest, once owned by a sailor called Edmund, had a story attached: 'When Edmund was away at sea he was convinced his wife was having an affair –

which led him to believe that his son was not his.' The Phoenix Group had

a vigil and were sure that the unexplained activities would then cease.

WALTON PRISON TALES

In order that we might understand just how much potential there is in a paranormal account of prison manifestations, this story begins with an inconceivably horrendous botched hanging in Walton prison, a place abounding in ghost sightings. The spirits allegedly seen in the former death cell area may well include a certain Henry Dutton.

This is a story as much about the hangman as it is about the murderer he was supposed to send to the next world. Henry Dutton, an ironworker, had killed Hannah Henshaw, his wife's grandmother, and was due to be hanged in the precincts of Kirkdale Gaol on December 3, 1883. The problem was that the man charged with seeing him quickly into oblivion was Bartholomew Binns.

Binns was only in the office for a year, and was sacked. Later, he assisted the more competent Tommy Scott in 1900, but in his own 'annus horibilis' as hangman he was responsible for a few botched jobs. He had helped the very professional and successful William Marwood, from Lincolnshire, who had invented the more humane 'long drop' method which involved more skilful calculations of the drop/body weight ratio. But Binns did not learn much. There were several complaints from governors and clergy about Binns's work and he was politely asked to go. He had a moment of notoriety when he was written about as the man who hanged one of the Phoenix Park murderers, O'Donnell.

But poor Dutton was to be hanged by Binns at Kirkdale. He had hanged a man for the first time just a few weeks before (Henry Powell at Wandsworth) but Duttton was only the second in line for the tyro executioner

There was a special element of drama in the case, as two local journalists were to be present, and also Dutton had asked the chaplain to give the optional Condemned Sermon on the Sunday before the fatal hour. The sermon was given, covering three warnings that are surely totally irrelevant, if not insulting, to a condemned man: not to be drunk, not to allow a bad temper to possess you, and not to marry in haste. Unless these were likely to happen in the next world, the whole affair appears to be cruelly ironic. But in the very early hours of his last day on earth, Dutton had something to eat (cocoa, bread and butter) and took sacrament in the prison chapel.

At seven Binns arrived. For some odd reason, the governor would not allow Binns' assistant to enter Kirkdale. It was normal practice to have a hangman together with his assistant. But the prison bell began to toll at a quarter to eight and in haste, Dutton was brought to meet Binns and to be pinioned ready for the drop. Then, as the chaplain read some text concerning man's sins, the ritual walk to the scaffold began.

This final walk was in line with regulations: the chief warder led the way, followed by Dutton and two warders; then Binns was behind them, followed in line by a doctor, the under-sheriff and chaplain. So far so good. But then they reached the scaffold.

The drama came when Dutton was given the rapid final pinioning and strapping ready for the lever to be pulled; the clock for eight had not struck, and Binns walked to look at his victim, causing a rather nervous atmosphere. Dutton asked Lord Jesus to receive his soul. Then the clock struck, and the lever was pulled; Dutton dropped, but it was not a quick death.

The doctor looked down at the struggling man on the rope and said, 'This is poor work, he is not dead yet.' In a drop of almost seven and a half feet, the body spun and the man did not die for eight minutes. That was outrageously cruel by any standards. The doctor could see what the problem was: a very thick rope had been used (like a ship's hawser, the doctor said) and Dutton was very short, only five feet two inches. The result was what every hangman feared: slow strangulation rather than a snapping of the spinal column with speed and humane intention.

There was an inquest after all this farce. Mr Barker, the County Coroner. The prison governor, Major Leggett, made a long statement outlining the time taken for the culprit to die, and also added that nothing had been done to 'hasten the end' of the unfortunate Dutton. The doctor's evidence would make difficult reading for anyone concerned about the terrible suffering the man had experienced: only a slight separation of two bones in the vertebrae near the point of contact with the rope had happened, rather than any sharp break. In the doctor's opinion, the noose had been placed at the wrong position near the nape of the neck, rather than under the jaw or the ear. There was, it was stated, a difference of 300 pounds in weight in the drop/body ratio.

The question that must have been on everyone's lips was boldly asked by the coroner: 'Was the executioner sober?'

Major Leggett answered that he was not sure. Then this interchange took place: something that must have ensured Binns' departure from his post:

Coroner: Has the hangman left the gaol?

Leggett: Yes

Coroner: I wish he were here

A juryman asked the governor's opinion of the affair. Leggett said, 'I think it was inefficiently performed-clumsily. I did not like his manner of conducting the execution. He seemed, in adjusting the strap on the man, to do it in a very bungling way, which I did not like at all.'

It was one of the most disgraceful cases of a botched execution in the annals of that grim but necessarily professional task at that period. As Shakespeare said in another context, 'If it were done, 'tis good it were done well.' The coroner considered the affair to have been a disaster, referring to the fact that 'the executioner seemed to be a new hand at the work' and that he should have done what the previous man, Calcraft, had done, that is pull on the legs of any man dangling but not swiftly dying.

One final irony in the Binns story is that he took part in a show featuring ex-hangmen, and that, as one writer of the time said, he 'reveals his art for the entertainment of the large crowds...' Incompetence was not to deter Mr Binns from making his year's deadly work the stuff of a media circus. The death cell, along with the notorious cell G2 which also housed a killer who was strung up, are places of intense paranormal energies. But the only problem with that story is that the man in question, Kennedy, who was supposed to be a police killer, was not hanged at Liverpool. It seems likely that there was some confusion about the man in the cell: it is more likely to have been James Winstanley, who murdered Edith Wilkinson. If there is a tormented soul in those walls, who can doubt the theory that it is Henry Dutton?

The condemned cell and 'execution suite' were revised four years after Dutton's death, as a new pit was made, providing a drop into which the condemned could fall, rather than mounting steps; a trap door was made as part of the death chamber.

Another case from history that may relate to sightings of a woman around the death cell is the notorious crime history of two sisters whose story relates to life insurance. There has been life insurance in Britain since 1762 when the Equitable Society started the first business. But there were always problems for the early companies, such as the fraud experienced by the Albion, founded in 1805, and the Eagle, started in 1807. It was only when the actuaries came along, and Milne's Mortality tables were printed in 1815 the way was open for smaller, working class companies to start business in the new rabbit-warren streets of the new industrial towns. The Institute of Actuaries was formed in 1848, and from that point there was always going to be the possibility that persons with a vested interest in a relative's death would break both the law and the moral code.

With that in mind, it is unbelievable how easy two Liverpool sisters found it to take out insurance on their family victims: they were killers, with a fondness for using poison. This murderous habit was to lead them both to the Kirkdale Gallows. Their story was a huge media sensation, with a high-profile trial, and even to the creation of their effigies at Madame Tussaud's Chamber of Horrors.

Horrible is the correct adjective to use for what Margaret Higgins and Catherine Flanagan did in 1883. That period was a busy one for the Liverpool police: in 1884 there were almost seven thousand people arrested in the city for being drunk and disorderly. In the Catholic slums of the north of the city, around Blenheim Street where the sisters lived, the labouring men lived a tough life, and for many it was a short life. That bare fact opens up the potential for types such as these sisters to exploit the life insurance system. So many people died of such illnesses as dysentery or fever that anyone who had been poisoned with arsenic could only really be spotted by a very astute doctor, and the medical men working in those streets would be working long hours and suffering from the stresses and strains of that work.

The tale begins with the women: both daughters of an Irish labourer, and born in Ireland; dates are uncertain but Angela Brabin estimates that Catherine was born around 1829 and Margaret around 1843. Catherine had lived in various houses in this area for over twenty years when she was arrested and interviewed in 1884. Her family was typical of so many working class families in the area: taking in lodgers, frequently moving house, and living a shiftless, vulnerable life in poor conditions. Catherine's family and lodgers consisted of her own son and daughter; a lodger called Jennings and his daughter; Peter Flanagan; another lodger called Rimmer and her sister, the widowed Margaret Thompson.

Catherine was a widow too: her husband John had died a few years before the story begins. He seems to have died of pneumonia but we have to be suspicious, given later events. But we should recall that Catherine was a survivor: she was managing to exist in reasonable comfort, even doing work as a money-lender, living and dressing well. The younger sister appears to have lost her husband in mysterious circumstances, but all traces of his death have gone. In 1881, she was living with her sister and described as a 'charwoman.' The team was ready to act then, when they set about ending the life of the first victim. There were probably ten known victims, but these are the accounts of the main four victims identified by the researcher Angela Brabin. Thomas Higgins comes first. Thomas, described by the Home Office as 'an Irish hodman of the lowest class', was a lodger with Catherine from around 1882. He came there with his wife and daughter - to 31, New Blenheim Street. They had not been there long when his wife died, and he then married Margaret Flanagan. In November, Flanagan's daughter died. Death was already becoming a regular event in the little world around the sisters.

When the whole group of family and lodgers moved house, this time to Ascot Street, Thomas himself died just after that move. Here was a man who had witnessed the deaths of his wife and daughter, under the roof of these sisters, and he had been approached to have life insurance taken out on his own life. Even when he began to experience the same nasty and painful symptoms that he had seen in his family, he does not seem to have acted. There was plenty of evidence about the nature of his illness and death, mainly from a neighbour, Catherine Manville. She made a statement before the coroner on 14 December, 1883.

In this statement, she recalled that both sisters had reported on how ill Higgins was, and that Catherine had been asked to come and see him. Her memory of the sick man was expressed powerfully: 'He was in bed. He seemed to be in great agony. He was facing the wall and moaning and scratching the wall with his fingers of both hands.' She returned later and then, 'The deceased put his hand on his breast and said "Oh if this pain had gone from me...,Äù he appeared to me to be very bad and suffering much...'

Higgins took a while to die. And there was some discussion in court about some liquid thrown into the fire-back. The issue was whether it contained brandy, or something more sinister. Dr Whitford had come to see the patient; he put the cause down to 'bad drink.' There was the smell of drink on his breath and he did say that he had been on the bottle.

Even when the man lay dying, the sisters and their neighbour discussed insurance. This is where we begin to understand the heartless and iniquitous core of this terrible crime. Margaret Higgins was given money by the insurance company after this, and what the sisters did when planning a murder was to try to obtain multiple polices of different kinds; for instance, this one was done under a rule from the British Workmen's Association with a ceiling of £20 (done without a medical). Margaret was the one who performed the grief-stricken wife in this business.

All this meant that sums received on their victims' lives varied considerably. For Thomas they received sums from three companies, totalling £108, though not all of this was paid out. This was a very large sum for a working class family at the time. In court, what became a centre of attention was the ease with which policies could be taken out, and the frequency of policies being approved by senior staff at these small firms.

One fact at the centre of all this was the previous physical robustness and good health of the man who had died; he was known by his peers as 'Crack the whip' and he was very strong. It was Flanagan's brother, Patrick, who played a major role on arousing general suspicion about the death. He asked around at the burial clubs and small insurance firms in the city. It was when Patrick actually brought Dr Whitford with him to see the body that something very underhand was suspected; the man had died from arsenic poisoning, not dysentery.

From that point, the backstory emerges, as other bodies were exhumed. First Mary, Higgins's daughter, was studied by Dr Lowndes, the police surgeon. It was clear from this that despite details about her suffering from pneumonia, the cause of death was probably arsenic poisoning; there was evidence from discolouration in her stomach and from the preservative action of the poison in some organs. There was no evidence of any insurance policy on her, and after interrogations, it was Margaret Higgins who was tried for the murder.

Then came Maggie Jennings, only eighteen years old. This 'strong, healthy girl' as her father described her, started feeling very unwell after eating dinner on 14 January, 1883. The poor man heard his daughter vomiting grievously, and it seems that the sisters took over beside duties and as the father later said, he was 'prevented by Mrs Flanagan' from seeing her. A doctor came to see her – this time a new man called Rafter – and he was confused and not up to doing much except that this was yet another case of pneumonia in Liverpool's unhealthy lodging houses. Once again, the sisters put on the caring and concerned act, seeming to be competent carers and then, when victims were in severe decline, they acted as though they were terribly distraught. This gave medical men like Rafter a certain confidence in leaving these killers alone with the patients, thus ensuring that the sick-bed would become the death-bed.

The last certain victim was from years before, and he was exhumed in January 1884. His body had been in Ford cemetery since December, 1880. This was the son of Catherine Flanagan, a young man of twenty-two who had been 'entered into clubs' just a few weeks before he died. The same conclusions came from the examination as had applied to young Maggie:

organs well preserved and no indications of a bronchitic condition which would have caused death (as was on the death certificate). A chemist, Edward Davies, found a great deal of arsenic in the liver. At the time of the death, his mother had put it about that her son had been killed by Catherine Flanagan, and the latter had actually taken out a suit against her for slander. With her usual skill of obtaining cash by not working for it, the killer received £5 from this.

In her confession, Flanagan said that 'My son John followed and he was insured by me but Higgins poisoned him and got a share of the money.'

The trial was sensational, of course, as it brought out a long-standing trade in insurance fraud and downright wilful murder in this community. Questions were asked about the whole business of 'poisoning rings' in such places, and also about the process and probity of the small firms undertaking insurance and burial club work

The sisters' exit from the world was also big news. One reporter at the time summed up the public feeling: 'The thought that these women had sent their nearest kith and kin into untimely graves after slow agonies of torture by poisoning should, perhaps, have enabled the most sensitive heart to regard their richly deserved fate with indifference.'

Their fate was recounted as graphically as their crimes; Higgins was terrified and heard nothing of the chaplain's supposedly comforting words, whereas her sister 'required little assistance to reach the scaffold.'

Higgins went to the rope with terrors of death upon her. Could it be her

A typical execution site in a Victorian prison Old print c.1890

shade that has been seen walking solemnly on the wing near the old death suite? There have been oral historical statements about a woman 'with her hair in a sort of bun' walking with her head down, towards the old death cell area.

ND - #0313 - 270225 - C0 - 234/156/11 - PB - 9781780914183 - Gloss Lamination